WHATCHAGOT STEW

ALSO BY PATRICK F. McMANUS

WHATCHAGOT
STEW

Illustrations by Shannon McManus Bayfield

Patrick F. McManus
& Patricia *"The Troll"* McManus Gass

A Memoir of
an Idaho Childhood,
with Recipes and Commentaries

Henry Holt and Company   New York

To John

Copyright © 1989 by Patrick F. McManus
All rights reserved, including the right to reproduce
this book or portions thereof in any form.
Published by Henry Holt and Company, Inc.,
115 West 18th Street, New York, New York 10011.
Published in Canada by Fitzhenry & Whiteside Limited,
195 Allstate Parkway, Markham, Ontario L3R 4T8.

Library of Congress Cataloging-in-Publication Data
McManus, Patrick F.
Whatchagot stew: a memoir of an Idaho childhood,
with recipes and commentaries / Patrick F. McManus—1st ed.
  p. cm.
ISBN 0-8050-0922-1
1. Cookery, American. 2. Cookery—Humor. I. Gass, Patricia
McManus, 1927– . II. Title.
TX715.M4746 1990
641.5973—dc20   89-11017
                                                CIP

Henry Holt books are available at special discounts
for bulk purchases for sales promotions, premiums,
fund-raising, or educational use. Special editions
or book excerpts can also be created to specification.

For details contact:
Special Sales Director
Henry Holt and Company, Inc.
115 West 18th Street
New York, New York 10011

First Edition

Designed by Lucy Albanese
Printed in the United States of America
10 9 8 7 6 5 4 3 2 1

CONTENTS

ACKNOWLEDGMENTS

We would like to give a special thanks to Bud and Josephine Hanson for letting us use some recipes from Uncle Ralph Hanson's personal cookbook, handwritten in 1930.

Most of the sourdough recipes are from Elvera V. Klein, author of *Creative Sourdough Recipes*. Copies of her book are available from Mrs. Klein, 284 West Carter St., Boise, ID 83706, for $4.95, plus $1.00 postage and handling.

We also wish to thank our friends, neighbors, and family for contributing recipes and suggestions for this book, and particularly Darlene McManus, for all her typing, editing, and good advice.

Clifford Arnzen	Paul Croy	Ralph and Verda Hanson
Kenneth Arnzen	Vic DeMers	Nancy Hobbs
Margaret Best	Charlie Elliott	Lucille Hudon
Roger Best	Harvey Felten	Gareth Johnson
Dorothy Bowen	John Gass	Genevieve Klatt
Sherry Colepaw	Mike and Theresa Gass	Gram Klaus
Nan Compton	Shaun and Carol Gass	Florence Lichter
Kim Cox	Connie Greenleaf	Sylvester Lukezich

Willy Madsen
Gladys O'Meara
Steve and Penny Runyan
Ross Russell
Bob and Idelle Schranck

Gary and Ann Skordahl
Lynn Spear
Jan Stolz
Florence Sulzle
Mae Van Derpas

Kelly Walkup
Isobel Weingardt
Jim and Lois Zumbo

PREFACE

Back about 1969, I came across one of those scary statistical articles in the newspaper. It predicted that within twenty years one out of every four people in the United States would either have written a cookbook or be a carrier.

I wasn't worried about myself, because I didn't belong to the high-risk group—people who cook. No more immune to self-delusion than the next man, I thought, It can never happen to me. The closest I'd ever come to cooking was opening a can of sardines. Sure, I was interested in food, but only in the eating of it. The article stated flatly that you can't contract cookbook writing merely from eating food; you actually have to come into physical contact with cooking. It did warn, however, that even the use of condiments is not 100 percent safe.

That worried me a little, because during my wild and reckless youth I had sprinkled both salt and pepper to excess. Everyone in my crowd was doing salt and pepper. In those days, you could scarcely get invited out to dinner without finding salt and pepper shakers on the table. So I fell into the habit of "shaking." I didn't think much about it for ten years or so. Then in October of 1980, I went to dinner at Bob and

Idelle Schranck's in Minneapolis. While Bob bustled happily about the kitchen, Idelle took me aside and whispered tearfully that within a few months Bob had gone from learning to boil water to actual cooking and now was engaged in writing a cookbook. She said he was at that very moment "cooking up" a recipe to test on us—his Pheasant Italiano.

"Pheasant Italiano," I said. "Sounds delicious."

"Don't ever let him hear you say that!" Idelle hissed. "It will only encourage him."

"He's that bad?"

"Yes!"

With great fanfare at dinner, Bob served his Pheasant Italiano, fixing me with an expectant grin as I took a bite. My taste buds instantly melted into euphoria. Never before had they known such ecstasy.

"Like it?" Bob asked.

"Not bad," I said. "Could use a little salt and pepper, though."

"Oh yeah," he snarled. "Well, maybe you should write your own damn cookbook, how about that?"

It's odd how little offhand suggestions plant themselves in some remote but fertile recess of the brain and begin to grow, undetected by the host organism until it's too late.

By 1985, the dire predictions of 1969 had come to pass. One out of every four persons in the United States was now either a cookbook writer or a carrier. Their numbers were growing exponentially. Carl Sagan wrote in *Parade* magazine that unless a serum was developed soon, within a few years all the land surface on earth would be covered with cookbooks to a depth of twelve feet. "There will be billions and billions of them," Sagan wrote, "until the supply of known recipe reserves is totally exhausted and the writers will be reduced to stealing each other's recipes and merely changing the names. Cooks will prepare 'Chicken Bombay' only to discover that it is the same as the old 'Chicken Kiev.' Chaos will reign!" Sagan named the impending catastrophe "The Soufflé Effect."

One day a couple of years ago, I was flying to Chicago on a business trip. Suddenly, I broke out in a cold sweat. This caused the gentleman seated next to me also to break out in a cold sweat, and he immediately began inventorying the plane's engines and running an intense visual examination of the seams in the passenger cabin. Satisfied that everything was in order, he asked, "What's the matter, pal? You sick or what?"

"I'm not sure," I said. "I just got this strange urge to write a cookbook."

The man excused himself to go to the rest room and did not return. I later saw him seated in the back of the plane hiding behind a copy of *Fortune*. I couldn't blame him. I would have done the same thing myself.

My urge to write a cookbook increased day by day, which was peculiar. I didn't know how to cook. I didn't want to learn to cook. I had never even read a cookbook. Why on earth did I feel this compulsion to write one? True, there was a certain amount of peer pressure. Most of my friends had written their own cookbooks, including *Tennis Players' Cookbook*, *Golfers' Cookbook*, and the hugely successful *Steel Workers' Cookbook*. I asked my therapist about the compulsion. He said there was no known cure for the malady, but he'd sell me an autographed copy of his *Schizoid Manic-Depressives' Cookbook*. I finally decided to write a cookbook and get it out of my system.

The first step was research. I called up my sister, Patricia Gass, and asked her to gather up all our old family recipes, prepare and test them, and write them out in cookbook form. Patricia said she was already writing her own cookbook.

"That's even better," I said. My exhaustive culinary research was proving easier than I had expected. "We'll call it *The McManus Cookbook*."

"No way," she said.

"We can't very well call it *The Gass Cookbook*, can we now?"

"I suppose not. By the way, what are you contributing to this project?"

"Oh, I'll toss in some of my own recipes—Roast Wiener on a Willow Stick, that old elk-camp favorite, Green Hash, and my Fried Bacon Flambé, and, uh, oh yeah, my famous Whatchagot Stew."

"What's Whatchagot Stew?"

I explained how, on a hunting trip, a bunch of us hunters happened to meet on a mountaintop. Everyone was ravenous, but we had already consumed most of our grub. "I know," I said, "we'll make us a communal stew."

"What'll we make it with?" Retch Sweeney asked.

"Whatchagot?" I asked the other hunters.

Vern had a couple of raw potatoes and an onion. Kenny had half a Big Mac he'd been saving for a snack. Norm had a couple of doughnuts. Keith had some smoked salmon. Bill had a candy bar and a package of Twinkies. I had some leftover Green Hash. Ross had a can of beets. And so on. We just tossed in whatever anyone had left in their grub box or kicking around on the floor of the truck. Then we boiled it all in a big pot of water for an hour to kill any taste. It was surprisingly edible, although in the future, I think I would omit the beets and probably the wool glove that turned up in the bottom of the pot. One or the other gave me a touch of indigestion.

"Maybe we should call my cookbook *Whatchagot Stew*," I told the Troll. "That way we can just toss in whatever we've got lying about and don't have to worry about some dumb theme. Doesn't that sound good?"

"First of all," Patricia said, "it isn't your cookbook. You'll have to contribute something to it, and we both know you can't cook."

"How can you say I'm not contributing anything?" I snapped. "Right now I'm working my ear to the bone researching the darn thing. What more can I do?"

"You could write a memoir of your Idaho childhood. How about that?"

"Hey, great idea!" I said. "I've always wanted to write a

memoir! I can write a wonderful memoir! How do you spell 'memoir'?"

So that is how I came to write a memoir of my Idaho childhood for this cookbook.

My memoir is pretty much true. Oh sure, occasionally I'll work in a little fiction for a change of pace and to relieve the monotony. (It's not as if I were Winston Churchill, you know.) If I stick to the unembellished truth for too long at a stretch, I tend to tense up, get a headache, and sometimes even break out in a rash. I have tried, however, to keep bald-faced lies well within the quota established by other writers of memoirs.

As you will see, this memoir is dominated by my mother. Mom would expect no less. After all, she dominated me, my sister, and the other members of the family, assorted relatives, neighbors, her pupils in school, parents of her pupils, and occasional strangers just passing through. She imposed her will on bankers, lawyers, doctors, priests, criminals, madmen, lawmen, several saints, automobiles, animals wild and domestic, earth and water, life and fate. Several times Death came for her too early, and she sent him away with his hat in his hand and apologizing profusely for having had the audacity to disturb her. Nor would she brook any nonsense from anything so tiny and silly as a cold germ; in the fifty years I knew her, she never once had a cold and considered it a flaw in the character of those who did. The only thing that remained immune to the force of Mom's will, as far as I know, was food. Even the simpleminded and cowardly potato rebelled, hurling back most of her assaults on it and refusing to be fried, baked, or boiled to any degree beyond the merely edible, and seldom that.

A word of warning: It would be a good idea for you to read the memoir first, before jumping into the recipes. Otherwise, out of ignorance, you might select one of my mother's recipes and foolishly even prepare and attempt to eat it, in the belief that because the recipe is included in a cookbook, it must be for something good to eat. The memoir will alert you to my mother's opportunistic and fatalistic approach to cooking. After that, you're on your own.

With the exception of a few of my contributions, all of the recipes in this book have been collected, invented, or stolen, as well as prepared and tested, by my sister and coauthor, sometimes referred to in this memoir as Patricia and at other times as Grendel the Troll, her childhood identity. Out of a sense of desperation and survival, Patricia became an excellent cook while she was still a young troll. She has had a keen interest in food all her life, not least when there was no food to be had. She is famous locally as a cook, and can whip out a scrumptious luncheon for six or a dinner for a hundred at the drop of a hint.

Many of the recipes belonged to my grandmother, a cook much sought after in the logging camps of northern Idaho, where the loggers were more concerned with the quality of the food in the camp than the quantity of dollars in their pay envelopes. Gram was a superb cook. The aroma of her baking alone could activate one's salivary glands at six hundred yards. When the wind was right, she could empty all the hoboes from a freight train and bring them streaming to our house for a handout. Only my dog, Strange, didn't care for Gram's cooking, and he complained to her constantly about it. His idea of a gourmet meal was a flattened roadkill, properly aged in a ditch for six months. (When I first heard of *The Roadkill Cookbook by* ———, I thought of Strange and how he would have enjoyed poring over the recipes.) My dog's criticisms of Gram's cooking, therefore, should not be taken seriously. I have also inserted recipes belonging to some of my hunting and fishing pals, and in one case, an entire wild-game dinner prepared by one of the great chefs of the Pacific Northwest, Willy Madsen.

Some people may become confused in reading this memoir as to the age of the Troll. I am one of those people. When we were children, she was much older than I. Now she is several years younger. I'm not sure how that works. The Troll claims that Einstein's theory of relativity explains the whole process. I have arbitrarily selected a date of birth for her, which may or may not be correct. Chivalry prevents my revealing the Troll's true age, and if anyone is so uncouth as to write me and insist upon learning it, I must warn that he runs the risk of being reported to Miss Manners. (Please enclose a self-addressed, stamped envelope.)

The Troll and I simmered our brains at a moderate temperature in an effort to come up with a theme for the recipes in this cookbook, without success. The only thing the recipes have in common is that they are for things we ate while growing up in Idaho, and later, and now. Many of them are simple but good. Others are complicated but good. Some are fattening but delicious. As I mention in the memoir, cholesterol didn't yet exist during the period we were children. (We had no environment or ecology back then either, which made life much simpler and safer.) I now discover that cholesterol has infiltrated some of these recipes to the extent that they can clog an artery at forty paces. You may wish to substitute ingredients of lower cholesterol content. On the other hand, what's a clogged artery or two when you're having fun?

I would at this time like to withdraw a statement I once made to the effect that writers of childhood memoirs are ego-centric, pretentious, and lying bores who only out of sheer arrogance could presume that anyone might care a flying fig about their pitiful and tedious memories of childhood. Surely, I jested.

A MEMOIR

I was born either August 24 or August 25, 1933. I have arbitrarily picked August 25 to celebrate, because that is the date on my birth certificate. All my life my birthday has been celebrated on August 25, even though my mother claimed that I was actually born on August 24. "But because your birth certificate has August twenty-fifth on it," she once explained to me, "I figured, what the heck, we might as well go with that."

The confusion over my birth date apparently arose out of the circumstances of my humble debut on the stage of life. I was born in a bedroom of our old farmhouse in the Panhandle of Idaho—near the top of the handle, about where you would grab it if you had to snatch a hot pan off the stove. The more-or-less attending doctor, for some reason unknown to me, came not from the town of Sandpoint, three miles away, but from a town thirty-five miles away. Maybe he was running a special on home deliveries. In any case, he turned out to be no bargain.

On the day in question, either the twenty-fourth or twenty-fifth of August, my father, Frank, arrived home with a couple of fifths of whiskey and started celebrating my imminent arrival. The doctor frequently emerged from the birthing bedroom to chat with Dad, a handsome and entertaining Irishman. "Join me for a drink, Doc?" Dad asked.

"Don't mind if I do," the doctor said. "But just one."

They killed the first fifth of whiskey to dull their labor pains, and started on the second just for the enjoyment of it. Naturally, I delayed being born as long as possible, with a prenatal sense that I had it pretty good where I was. The outside world was in the grip of the Great Depression. People were hungry and cold and out of work and nobody had any money, particularly for toys and candy. Hitler had come to power in Germany, and the faint but acrid odor of war was already in the air. A baby would have to be a fool to get himself born at such a time and, no fool, I resisted with all my might. My birth was hard on my mother but, according to her, not nearly so difficult as putting up with me as a kid. By the time I finally emerged into this pail of tears, kicking and screaming all the way, my father and the doctor had seriously maimed the second bottle of whiskey, if not killed it. Dad was in jovial good spirits, and I liked him right off. He seemed like my kind of guy. The doctor, on the other hand, appeared bleary and befuddled, and I am not surprised that he took a wild guess for a date to put on my birth certificate. According to Mom, he guessed wrong.

There was even some confusion over the doctor's fee. Mom told me once that she had paid the doctor off in home-canned

preserves. She said that after seeing how I had turned out, she figured she had been overcharged by at least two pints of dewberry jam and a quart of string beans. Many years later, when I mentioned the doctor's fee in a story, she denied ever having told me such a ridiculous thing. She now claimed she had paid the doctor off at the rate of five dollars a month "practically forever." I prefer the preserves version. Somehow it seems more fitting.

I was born into confusion and confusion has been my normal state of existence ever since. Generally speaking, it has served me well. I have always felt a little sorry for people who lead orderly lives. They miss so much of the excitement that comes from chaos and frenzy. I believe I have my mother to thank for introducing me to the finer aspects of confusion. She lived her whole life on the edge. On the edge of what, I don't know, nor do I wish to. We normally dwelt well down inside the existential abyss—with our backs to the wall—so it couldn't have been the edge of that.

My father was already dying of cancer when I was born. He had fought in the famous Rainbow Division during World War I, under the command of a young officer named Douglas MacArthur, whom he did not much care for. A dose of mustard gas may have been the cause of Dad's cancer. In the few grim years that I knew him, he drank heavily, often experiencing what is now referred to as delayed stress syndrome but which then was commonly referred to as "shell shock." We refought a number of World War I battles with him, and I have had a bad opinion of war ever since. Frequently, he was away in hospitals, or just away, and I have only half a dozen fond recollections of him.

I remember his once bringing me home a tin boat powered by steam generated from fat little brown candles. Dad stood about watching me fill a washtub with water in preparation for the launching. I noticed he had ripped open a little package and was munching the contents, occasionally plucking a string out of his teeth and complaining about the lack of flavor in the "candy." We soon discovered that Dad had eaten all the fuel for my steamboat. He thought it extremely funny, I less so. I never did find out if the steamboat actually worked. Furthermore, I have had trouble with boats ever since.

On another occasion, a rainy day in the woodshed in which we were temporarily living, Dad and I were spending some quality time together while my mother was off somewhere, probably trying to scrounge up dinner for us. To amuse me, Dad took a pencil and drew some bawdy cartoons on the wall.

I thought they were hilarious. Someone else owns that woodshed now, even uses it for a woodshed. I know those cartoons are still there, probably hidden behind a stack of wood, and I have often thought about stopping by and asking the family if they would mind my sawing a small section of wall out of their woodshed, for art's sake. That family has electricity, though, and the children probably get their cartoons from television on Saturday morning. It might be hard for the present owners to grasp the significance of the cartoons drawn on their woodshed wall, and I certainly would not want to explain it to them.

My mother was a rock—a rock sometimes crumbling about the edges and often slipping further down the wall of the abyss, but a rock nonetheless. A bark-hided old trapper once commented that Mom had more grit than any person he had ever known. The trapper, who had no shortage of grit himself, said it not as a compliment but as an expression of awe, shaking his head in wonderment at the massive quantities of grit in the character of one tiny woman. A rock, of course, is composed mostly of grit. It is also very hard.

My mother was born in Kirksville, Missouri, in 1900. Her parents, Pete and Edith Klaus, named her Mabel. In 1905, Pete filed on a homestead near Sandpoint, Idaho, built a claim shack about the size of a modern kitchen, and moved his family into it. The family now included Mabel's older sister, Gladys; a younger sister, Verda; and a baby brother, Gordon. Theirs was one of the more crowded claim shacks around. Pete started a logging operation and within a few years was making a substantial amount of money. He even added a lean-to onto the claim shack, a structure that stands to this day and serves the owner as a garden-tool shed. As a young Missouri farmer, my grandfather reportedly had been a gentle and quiet man. But something about Idaho—possibly the long, bitter winters—changed him. "He took to drink," my mother said, "and that was his downfall." Within a few years, ole Gramps developed a fearsome reputation in the saloons and logging camps of North Idaho.

I know only a couple of stories about my grandfather, but they give me some hint as to his character. One time he hired a woman cook for his logging camp. When she arrived in Sandpoint, the new cook apparently hadn't paid all of her fare, and the stage office manager refused to give up her luggage until she did so. She walked out to Pete's camp, borrowed a horse from him, and rode back to the stage office. She pulled a pistol, stuck it in the stage manager's face, and told him she would have her bags now. The manager didn't argue. Presently, the lady galloped back into camp on the foam-lathered horse and yelled at Pete that she had a posse hot on her tail. "Step down and hit for the timber," Pete said, not about to lose his cook before she had even cooked. "I'll handle the posse." A few minutes later the posse thundered up to find Pete wiping down the exhausted horse.

"Pete," the sheriff said, "a woman just held up the stage office and rode off hell-bent for destruction on a horse exactly like the one you're wiping down there. You seen her?"

"Nope," Pete said, "I ain't."

"You ain't?" the sheriff said, staring at the horse. "Well, if she turns up, let me know, okay?"

"You bet," Pete said.

The sheriff, seeing no reason to continue the pursuit beyond Pete's camp, took his posse back to town.

I have gathered from this story that my grandfather was not a man to be trifled with, especially over so minor a thing as a holdup. As far as his new cook was concerned, Pete believed it fair and reasonable for a lady to take by force what rightfully belonged to her. He changed his mind, however, after she cooked her first meal for his crew. Upon attempting to bite into one of her biscuits, he saw right away that he had done wrong in hiding a dangerous criminal from the sheriff. He felt bad about neglecting his civic duty and vowed to turn his cook over to the law at first opportunity. Reluctant to fire a woman, particularly one so handy with a pistol, Pete was considerably relieved when she quit after the first payday.

When Mabel was about eight years old, Pete took her and

her sister Gladys to town for the Fourth of July celebration. He gave them each a nickel and then headed for his favorite saloon. As soon as Mabel had blown her whole nickel, she went looking for Pete to get another one. She found him outside a saloon arguing with a man about a horse. The man claimed the horse was so wild that he was the only person who could ride it.

"Hell," Pete said, "my little girl could ride that horse."

"Bet you a drink," the man said.

Pete knew a sure bet when he saw one. He swept his little girl up onto the back of the horse, whacked the animal on the flank, and Mabel and the horse streaked out of town "like a burr on a turpentined dog."

Pete then strolled into the saloon to collect on his bet.

My grandmother finally had her fill of Pete's wild and wanton ways. She and the children packed up their few belongings and started walking to town. Whether my grandfather was secretly saddened by his family's departure seems unlikely. His only visible reaction, as related to me years later, was that he stood in the doorway of the claim shack and fired a .30/30 rifle repeatedly over their heads. Gram said she was just glad Pete was sober that day and in fairly good humor. Other than that, I can't recall her ever having a nice word to say about my grandfather.

Mabel was twelve years old when her mother divorced Pete. Gram hired on to cook at the Sandpoint hospital and kept Gordon and Verda with her. I'm not sure what Aunt Gladys did, but Mom struck out on her own. As a maid for the family of the district forest ranger, she worked her way through seventh and eighth grades and high school, after which she worked her way through teachers college. She loved school. Even though she had to walk three miles from the claim shack to grade school in all kinds of North Idaho weather, she won the award every year from first to sixth grade for never once being tardy or absent. She also got straight A's. School was her haven from chaos.

In the hospital, shortly before she died in 1987, Mom briefly withdrew from chaos and regressed once again into a happy and competitive grade-school girl. While I sat by her bedside, a weary young doctor walked in filling out a report of some kind. "What day is it?" he asked absently. Beaming girlishly, my mother raised her hand and waved wildly for the teacher's attention. As always, she knew the answer.

THE PLACE

*M*om never tired of telling my sister and me that because she had missed having a real home as a child (she always referred to the claim shack as the claim shack), she was going to make darn sure her own children had one. So shortly after she and my father were married, they bought the little farm where I was born. More stump ranch than farm, the land was covered with huge, fire-blackened stumps left over from the logging days—most of the valley looked as if it had been given a massive crew cut by the loggers. In addition to a good crop of stumps, the farm consisted of a barn, a chicken house, a root cellar, and a rather pleasant house surrounded by fruit trees and a picket fence. Sand Creek ran along the back edge of the farm, providing drink for the farm animals, gravel for the farm roads, ice for the icebox and ice-cream maker, a sandy beach for picnicking and swimming, and, for a while, an abundance of excellent fishing. As I understand it, the early years on The Place, as Mom always called the farm, were among the happiest of my mother's life. Each fall, Mom would go off to teach in the rural schools of North Idaho, and Dad would work in whatever mills or logging camps happened to be nearby. They seem to have danced, played cards, and generally partied almost continuously for the first few years of their marriage. They both loved a good time. Vacations and summers were spent at The Place. It was a time of joy and abundance, experienced briefly by my sister, who was born in 1927—on either August 30 or August 31.

The farmhouse burned down one night when I was four or five. It was the first time I recall witnessing my mother's wonderful talent for turning her back on disaster and plunging ahead into the future. As we stood in the flickering orange light of the flames devouring our home and watched some neighbor men frantically trying to save a few pieces of our furniture, I thought the world had come to an end. Then Mom said to my sobbing sister and me, "You know what? You see that grove of trees over there? We'll build a house in among the trees. It will have big windows to catch the morning light, and there will be lots of bedrooms, and a big kitchen, and even a bathroom! Doesn't that sound nice?" And she was actually smiling, her eyes shining with the light from the flames consuming her first and only home and nearly all of her possessions. If I had known having the house burn down would give her such joy, I would have torched the place myself. In fact, a fairly strong case was made that I had done just that, playing with matches.

The very next day after the fire, Mom went to town and mortgaged the farm to get money for the new house. While we camped out in the grove of trees, she had a woodshed built so we would have a place to live. Within a year, she had willed the new house into existence, and it was exactly the way she had described it the night of the fire. She paid off the mortgage at twenty dollars a month "practically forever."

THE TROLL

Frank and Mabel named their new baby girl Patricia Ann. They thought she was the most beautiful child they had ever laid eyes on. The family photo albums are gorged with photographs of her prancing about in cute little dresses, riding her pony, playing with her expensive toys. By contrast, in my senior year, when the staff of the high-school annual asked for a baby picture of me, not a single such picture could be turned up. Too embarrassed to admit that my parents hadn't taken a single picture of me as a baby, I substituted one of my cousin Don. Grilled by me as to why there were so many baby pictures of my sister and none of me, Mom said, "I can't remember. Probably we didn't have enough money to buy film. There was a depression on, you know. Nobody had any money."

"I know why," Patricia said. "It was because you were such an ugly baby!"

"But he was a good baby," Mom said kindly. She thought my desperate and fruitless seach for a single baby picture of myself extremely funny. My mother had a strange sense of humor. Her strange sense of humor probably played a part in naming my sister Patricia and me Patrick, so that there would be two Pat McManuses in the family, one of the sources of the endless confusion with which I would become so well acquainted.

Although she never had it tested, my mother's IQ must have soared into the stratosphere. She was a whiz at math. Once when she was a tottering old lady, my nephew Mike, a Ph.D., was explaining one of his projects to her and happened to mention an equation of some sort. "Why, that can't be right, Mike," she said. "It must be thus and so." Mike sat down and worked out the equation for her with pencil and paper. And Mom was right. It was a humbling experience for Mike. I was all too familiar with such humbling experiences. Intellectually, Mom could strike your ego like a bolt of lightning and leave it crisp and smoking and curled up around the edges. She always thought I was "a little slow," as she graciously put it. She never came right out and said "dumb." Unfortunately, it was my sister who inherited the high-IQ gene from my mother, once breezing through two grades in a single year. By the time I came along, the IQ gene had already been wasted on my sister, and I had to make do with the leftovers.

It is a terrible thing for a boy to have to grow up with a sister who is not only beautiful (in the opinion of her father and mother) but smart. Because she was six years older, Patricia was also a good deal stronger than her little brother. One of the great joys of her life was to torment me into a maniacal rage in which I would lose all sense of self-preservation and hurl myself at her in a suicidal assault. She would throw me to the floor, sit on my chest, grab one of my hands, and fiendishly grind the knuckles together until I howled satisfyingly.

"Shut up that howling and leave your sister alone," Mom would yell from somewhere in the house.

My sister's store of torments seemed endless. On the rare occasions that candy bars were bought for us, I would wolf mine down, and Patricia would make a pretense of eating hers. Days later, when I was ravenous for candy, she would bring her Hershey bar out of hiding and, smacking her lips out of all proportion to the treat, nibble one of the tiny squares mere inches from my drooling lips and pleading eyes. She could make a single candy bar last upward of three miserable weeks. In all honesty, I must confess that she once succumbed to my begging and gave me a piece of her gum. What surprised me most was that it still retained quite a bit of flavor.

I have always had a weak stomach, particularly in regard to soft-fried eggs. When Patricia discovered this chink in my gastronomical armor, it was as though she had found the Holy Grail. She devised dozens of truly disgusting things to do with her fried eggs at the breakfast table, but with a subtlety that concealed her efforts from my parents. Even I had to study her closely to detect exactly what she was doing to nauseate me. I would complain, but to no avail. Then one day she overreached herself, going beyond the limits of mere disgust and into the realm of the truly sick. My father smacked her a good one, causing me to break out in a smile that lasted for hours. Turned out Dad, too, had a weak stomach. Her wretched little game had been found out, and from that day onward, whenever fried eggs were served, I was allowed to build a barrier of cereal boxes to protect me from the sight of my sister.

During one of our more deadly battles, she threw me down on a double-bitted ax, which narrowly missed my throat and cut my chin open. I still have the scar to prove it. Years later my mother recalled the event with some amusement. "I can't believe you would actually throw your little brother down on an ax and cut his chin like that," she said to my sister. "What was the problem anyway?"

"Bad aim," Patricia said, "mostly bad aim." She and Mom chuckled appreciatively.

When I started writing stories about my childhood, I referred to my sister as "the Troll." I had in mind Grendel, the monstrous troll in *Beowulf*, who murderously ravaged the warriors of Hrothgar, king of the Danes. Grendel seemed a fitting model for my sister, but I was afraid the connotation of the name would escape many of my readers. An unhappy result of the use of "the Troll" in my stories is that many of my young male readers now refer to their innocent female siblings by that name, and I now regret having called my sister "the Troll." Probably I should have gone with "Grendel," as I had first intended.

I should mention here that my sister disagrees totally with this account of our childhood conflicts, particularly as to who was the tormentor and who the tormentee. In reply, I can only say, "Whose memoir is this, anyway?"

If it were the Troll's memoir, she would probably mention something about my having put an innocent little garter snake in her underwear drawer. I should like to point out that nothing was ever proved as to my guilt in the matter. Anyone could have slipped the snake in there. Maybe it was my grandmother, or my dog, Strange. We often had hoboes stopping by the house for a handout. One of them could have done it. Maybe the snake got in the drawer by itself. There are any number of possibilities. Why the Troll should hurl her unfounded accusations at me, I don't know. Fortunately, people aren't going to pay serious attention to the ravings of a person who goes through life forking her underwear out of a drawer with a long stick.

SQUAW VALLEY

*I*n 1939, when I was six, the school year was about to start, and Mom was still without a teaching job and therefore without money. Her big worry was how she would buy my sister and me winter coats. The more serious and immediate problem, however, was that I had no clothes with which to start first grade at the Farmin School in Sandpoint, a school where the playgrounds were governed not so much by supervisors but by the rule of social Darwinism: survival of the fittest, or possibly of the fleetest. My grandmother, bless her heart, said, no problem, she would sew me up a pair of pants. She then set to work creating one of the most hideous garments ever to offend the sensibilities of a small but macho boy—baggy, black-wool, knee-length shorts held up by straps over the shoulders! Naturally, I refused even to try on such a sartorial abomination, vowing they would have to kill me first. But I was going up against two of the most strong-willed women I have ever known. I would have stood more chance defying General George S. Patton backed up by Genghis Khan. My threats were swept aside as if but flakes of unsightly dandruff. I was no match for Mom and Gram. As I emerged from the school bus on the first day of school, the playground ruffians stared at my black woolen shorts in astonishment and delight. Here, truly, was a specimen worthy of their talents for torment. It was an opportunity that they had long dreamed of but never expected to occur within their lifetimes. My sister, Troll, age twelve, instantly and loudly disavowed any knowledge as to the possible identity of the small, bizarrely dressed creature attempting to cling to her for protection. She shrugged me off and disappeared into the anonymity of the gathering crowd of interested spectators. And then the ruffians were upon me. I have hated school ever since.

After a mere but memorable two weeks in first grade, I got sprung, one of the happiest moments of my life. Mom belatedly was offered a job teaching the Squaw Valley school.

I now realize that most of the backwoods schools my mother taught in were wretched places, but the most wretched of all was the Squaw Valley school, an ancient, single-room log structure rotting away in a picturesque mountain valley thirty miles north of Priest River, Idaho. (Mom commented once that the only thing that could send some of the mountain people to town was the opportunity to vote against a school-bond issue.) In addition to teaching all eight grades—about forty different lessons a day—Mom's job included chopping the firewood and kindling, building and maintaining the fire in the rusted-out barrel stove, cooking and serving the "hot lunch," hauling drinking water in a bucket from nearby Goose Creek (which, in winter, required chopping a dipping hole through the ice), producing programs for Christmas and other holidays, and serving as the hostess for all the community social functions at the school in the evenings, mostly dances and card parties. For this, she was paid $85 a month. She could scarcely believe her good fortune.

We lived right in the school's one room, our beds behind the rows of seats. I saw right away that it would be absolutely useless for me to stay home sick in bed, because I would still be in school anyway. Otherwise, the setup looked pretty good to me. I was already well accustomed to such a school. Day-care centers having not yet been invented when I was born, my mother simply hauled her new baby into the schoolrooms with her, stashing me in a corner with a few crayons, first to chew on, and later to color the pictures she sketched out to keep me occupied. My having been pretty much a mobile fixture in her previous schools, coming and going as I pleased, may have been the reason Mom didn't seem to realize that I was now supposed to be one of her pupils in first grade. I would get up and wander outside anytime I felt like it, which was often. Not only did my mother not frown on this practice, she didn't even seem to notice. Upon my return, she might ask, "What have you been up to?"

"Catchin' frogs in the crick," I'd reply.

"That's nice," she'd say. "Don't bring them inside."

This routine continued not only through the year I was supposed to be in first grade at Squaw Valley, but also through the year I was supposed to be in second grade. It was marvelous!

No matter how much fun I might be having outside of school at Squaw Valley, I always tried to get back in time for the noon reading. After lunch each day, Mom read aloud from one of her favorite books, among which were those of Mark Twain and Jack London. She was a wonderful reader and seemed to enjoy *The Adventures of Huckleberry Finn* or *The Call of the Wild* as much as her young audience, even though it was her tenth time through the novels. Fiendishly, she contrived to end each day's reading at a moment of unbearable suspense. I think this was a device to lure some of her more reluctant students back to school the following day. It worked with me, at least as far as the noon reading was concerned. I eventually became so frustrated with having to wait until the next day to find out how the characters escaped their predicament that I taught myself to read. I have always lacked patience.

Teaching myself to read used up the better part of a day. Over the years, I had absorbed phonics subliminally merely by hanging out in the classroom. I knew all the sounds for the letters and most of the combinations of letters. So I snatched a third-grade reader off a shelf, sat down on my bed and began sounding out the first story, something about the growing of peanuts. For hours I sounded my way through the story, finally reaching the end but with little comprehension of what I had sounded through. I started over. The content of the text slowly began to emerge, and I realized that I was reading something less than a red-hot page turner. Again I sounded through the story, beginning to recognize many of the words. My body and head were wracked with pain from the effort. Still, I persisted. And by the end of the day, I could read the story perfectly, comprehending once and for all that peanuts grow underneath the ground like potatoes and not on top of it like peas, as I had supposed. It was the most boring story I had ever encountered.

At supper that evening, I made my triumphant announcement to Mom. "Guess what!" I said. "I learned to read today!"

"That's nice," she said. "Now eat your gruel."

SPIRITS

I didn't realize until I was six years old that my father, mother, and sister were devout Catholics, because we never went to church. As a result, I was somewhat confused one Sunday when we all drove down from Squaw Valley to Priest River to attend Mass. I sat patiently on the hard pew staring up at the altar in anticipation, waiting for something to happen. Minutes ticked by as my mother and father did their best to give the impression that they were regulars in attendance at Sunday Mass, in some other parish, of course. Finally, I could stand it no longer and blurted out loudly to my father, "When does this show get started, anyway?"

Still embarrassed from my having blown his cover, Dad noticed during the sermon that I was wiggling loose one of my baby teeth, blood dribbling gruesomely down my chin. He reached out in an effort to pull my hand away from my mouth just as the tooth came loose, and his hand knocked it skidding away under the pews in front of us. I was not about to abandon that tooth, which was worth at least a dime from the tooth fairy. I lunged after it, crawling under several pews and fighting my way through a forest of legs. Dad came after me, trying to grab one of my feet and haul me back. Just as I saw the tooth mere inches from my outstretched hand, Dad got hold of my foot. I grabbed a couple of handy legs and fought to hold my position. We struggled savagely. Around us, the murmurs of the faithful rose in volume, all but drowning out the pastor's sermon and my father's angry snarls. Dad

gave a mighty tug and the stocking of the lady whose leg I clutched suddenly slipped its garter snap and almost caused me to lose my grip. Frantic now, I made one last lunge and snatched up the precious tooth. I was so relieved I didn't even bother to scold my father when I returned to the pew. Dad didn't scold me either, although he did mutter on the way home that he intended to strangle the tooth fairy if he ever laid hands on her. I just hoped he would use some judgment and strangle her after she paid me for my tooth and not before. Timing is everything when you strangle a tooth fairy.

The tooth fairy was not the only spirit we had around. Although my parents seldom attended church in those years, largely because of the remote areas in which we lived most of the time, they were very religious and good Catholics in their peculiar way. They never ate meat on Fridays, for example, a sin not too difficult to avoid since they didn't eat meat many other days of the week either, but it was the thought that counted.

Now, the Catholic Church at that time forbade messing around with Ouija boards, and probably still does. Ouija boards are excellent things to forbid messing around with, and I would no more allow my children to touch a Ouija board than I would hand them a loaded gun to play with. I do not know what makes a Ouija board "work," but I know that it does. Whether it serves as a communications device for tapping into the spirit world or into the subconsciousness of its operators, I have no idea, but it taps into something with powerful intelligence and emotions, a keen and ingenious wit, and unknown motives. As a friend of mine who got involved with what is called "channeling" once commented, "Opening the 'door' is easy. But you never know what's coming through." He was too shaken up to mention what had come through the "door" he had opened up, but it must have been pretty bad. He gave up right on the spot a promising and perhaps profitable career in the channeling business.

Both of my parents had been involved with Ouija boards most of their lives. When she was a young girl, my mother had been told by a Ouija board that she would marry a tall dark handsome man with the initials F.M. Years later at a party, a tall dark handsome man asked her to dance, and while they were dancing she asked him his name. "Frank McManus," he answered. She knew right then that she had found her future husband.

Because messing with Ouija boards was forbidden by the Church, my parents adopted the attitude that the little board was merely an entertaining oddity that no sensible person would take seriously. Obviously, the Church, in forbidding the use of Ouija boards, only meant that they were not to be taken seriously. During a boring evening—most of our evenings were boring—one of them would say, "I know, let's play with the Ouija board." Then they would make a great show of what amusing nonsense they thought Ouija boards were. "Ho-ho, ha-ha-ha-ha," they would laugh, hauling the little wooden creature out of its hiding place.

The Ouija boards my parents used were not the commercial jobbies one occasionally now finds in toy departments, of all places, with the letters printed on a board for the Ouija to spell out its words with. (I came across one of the plastic kind once in a toy department when my wife was with me. Although she thought I was crazy when I said, "Let's test it," she cooperated. We both put the tips of our fingers on it, but before I could think of a question to ask the Ouija, the board began racing about from letter to letter. It spelled out "B-U-Y

M-E." So all right, scoff, see if I care.) My father whittled our Ouijas out of a piece of wood. Although I later whittled out many of them myself, I will not go into detail about the construction of the little contraptions, except to say that they were capable not only of writing out sentences in longhand with a pencil but could also draw pictures. It was a highly symbolic picture one once drew for a friend of mine—a disbeliever in the psychic power of a piece of wood—that caused me once and for all to sever all relationships with the Ouija. I believe it was Ralph Waldo Emerson who once said of such mystic matters, "One world at a time! One world at a time!" That's good enough for me. But it wasn't for my parents, whose present world wasn't all that great.

Dad and Mom would spread a sheet of butcher paper on the table, both of them chuckling all the time at this amusing nonsense, set the board on the paper, place the tips of their fingers on it, and begin asking the Ouija questions. The "spirit contact" was the same one, or at least had the same name, as the one who had told Mom as a young girl that she would marry a man with the initials F.M. There are few things more foolish looking than a couple of adults sitting at a table asking a little piece of wood questions. Dad and Mom were probably aware of this, so after every answer they would both laugh and joke, to show that they were merely having fun with this bit of nonsense, just in case spies of the Church might be peeking in the window and misinterpret the activity as a serious undertaking. As far as I could tell, my parents were not so much interested in news of the spirit world as they were of our present one—the mail and newspaper routes stopped thirty miles short of Squaw Valley and of course there was no phone. Pretty soon my parents would start asking the Ouija about living friends and relatives rather than dead ones, most of the latter reportedly having a better time of it than we were. "Ha-ha-ha," Mom would say, "how is Verda these days? Ha-ha-ha." The Ouija would answer, "Fine."

"Ha-ha-ha," Dad said to the piece of wood one evening.

"How is George getting along? Ha-ha-ha!" (George was a longtime boyfriend of my grandmother.)

"Dying," the piece of wood replied.

"Ha . . . *dying?*" Dad said. "I didn't even know George was sick."

"Good heavens!" Mom said. "We'd better go see him."

So much for their flimsy pretense that the Ouija was nothing more than a little amusing oddity. The next day we drove sixty miles over icy roads to Sandpoint, where we found George in the hospital, dying.

George's was the first deathbed I had ever visited. He was so weak that he could barely whisper. He was obviously trying to tell my parents something, but they couldn't make out what it was. They told me to put my ear up next to George's mouth to see if I could understand him. I did so.

"Can you make out what he's saying?" Dad asked.

"Yes," I said. "I think so. He says, 'Give . . . Pat . . . a . . . quarter.' "

No, only kidding about that, although it no doubt occurred to me. Actually, I couldn't understand what George was saying either. It was probably, "Get that kid's damn ear out of my mouth and let me die in peace." George and I never did get along too well.

My father delighted in a good practical joke, particularly one that scared the daylights out of the victim. Two young ranch hands would often come over to the school in the evening to play pinochle with Dad and Mom. To get to the school, they had to walk along a narrow trail through thick woods. The middle section of the trail passed along an eerie swamp, where a huge, deformed cedar tree reared up ominously close to the path. The big tree was imaginatively referred to as "the big tree." Buck and Wally, the two cowboys, were fascinated by the Ouija board, whose strange powers Dad had demonstrated to them. One night when they came to visit, Dad got my sister aside and told her what to make the Ouija write. It was such a mean and dirty trick that the Troll hesitated to go along with it, for two or three seconds. When Wally and the Troll took a turn at the Ouija, she pushed the board around, making it write, "Watch out for the big tree. Watch out for the big tree tonight."

"What do you suppose that means?" Wally said, looking around nervously.

"Gosh, I don't know," Dad said soberly. "Sounds like a warning of some kind. Maybe you boys should spend the night here."

"I think maybe I'll leave right now," Wally said, pulling his hat firmly down on his head in the manner of a man expecting a strong breeze. Even as he went out the door he was picking up momentum for the trip home. He said later that, just as he was passing the big tree, an owl hooted and took off flapping into the night. Wally said that must have been what the Ouija had been warning him about, because he nearly died of fright on the spot.

Buck, on the other hand, claiming he had no fear of spooks, stayed on at the school for a few games of pinochle. When it came time for him to leave, he decided that rather than go home by the trail, he would walk around by the road, which was a longer route by only about five miles. He explained that his reason for taking the longer way home was that he figured Wally would be hiding at the big tree, planning to leap out and scare him, and this would be a good trick on Wally. Nobody bought Buck's story. When Buck failed to show up at a reasonable time back at the ranch, Wally concluded that the spook, having missed him at the tree, possibly because of being unprepared for a victim traveling at such high speed, had leaped out and nabbed the slower and disbelieving Buck. Wally was still trying to get his hair to lie flat again when the exhausted Buck clumped through the door of the bunkhouse.

Sometimes the Ouija played practical jokes on my parents. A train was robbed near our place in the last century, and the bandits supposedly made off with a great deal of loot. They were caught, hanged, and tried, but the loot was never found. It was thought that they might have buried it in the general vicinity of our place. One night Dad said to the Ouija, "Ha-ha, is there any treasure buried on our place? Ha-ha?" The Ouija wrote: "In the old root cellar by the creek." This was the root cellar in which my mother stored her preserves. The next morning Dad got up early and Mom asked him what he was going to do that day.

"Oh, I thought I'd dig out the floor in the root cellar."

"That sounds like a good idea."

Dad not only dug out the floor of the root cellar, he practically turned it into a well. The cellar was ruined and no gold found. At one point the shovel hit some boards, and we all thought we were going to be rich. But the boards turned out to be boards. I don't recall my father laughing over the Ouija's little joke.

It was because of my parents' messing with the Ouija board that I grew up with a sense of spirits hovering about me, always ready to put in their two cents' worth. I know that they are calling me, but I refuse to pick up the phone. The call's probably collect anyway. On the other hand, it might just be my subconscious or, worse, Shirley MacLaine's. I agree with old Waldo—One world at a time! One world at a time!

We had saints around, too. Whenever Mom lost something, she would say a little prayer to Saint Anthony, the patron saint of lost things. Within a few minutes, a day at the latest, she would find whatever it was that she had lost. As far as I know, Saint Anthony never let her down.

"Lord, save us!" was my mother's favorite exclamation. We led such precarious lives that on a normal day she might shout it out two or three times, often in regard to our breakfast, lunch, or dinner bursting into flames on a hot stove. (One of her favorite culinary tips was, "Just scrape off the burnt part.") The Lord usually saved us, too. In fact, my mother called upon Him so often that I'm surprised He had time for anyone else. Driving our old car from Squaw Valley to Sandpoint, she might shout out, "Lord, save us!" a dozen or more times on a single trip. Sometimes we would all shout out the plea in unison. I'm not sure if the car had any brakes, but I know it didn't have any lights. Because Mom's top driving speed was something less than thirty-five miles per hour, half the drive was made in the dark without lights. The Lord's usual agent in saving us was Sheriff George O'Donnell. After several logging trucks had nearly squished our car flatter than a roadkilled rabbit and swerved out around us with blaring horns ("Lord, save us!"), the blinking red light of the sheriff's car would suddenly illuminate the interior of ours. The sheriff would walk wearily up to Mom's window. "Mabel," he would snarl in frustration, "you've just got to get those lights fixed!"

"Don't raise your voice to me, George," Mom would snap back. "I told you half a dozen times I'll get them fixed! Now what I want you to do is drive behind me and shine your lights ahead so I can see to drive the rest of the way home. It's the least you can do."

"All right, Mabel, all right! But get those lights fixed. This is the last time I'm gonna tell you." (Both he and Mom knew it wouldn't be the last time.) Then the sheriff would follow us all the way home at something scarcely exceeding the pace of a snail. I'm sure he was praying, "Lord, I can't keep answering your emergency calls to save Mabel and the kids. Please send me some help. I've got other work to do."

The most spectacular and immediate answer to one of Mom's prayers came one Christmas morning when, typically, there was no meat of any kind, let alone turkey or ham, available for dinner. She was teaching at a prairie school in Montana, and a blizzard had blocked all the roads to town. So Mom called the problem to the attention of God, and a short while later He sent a prairie chicken crashing through one of the school's windows. Mom had probably been expecting a plump ring-necked pheasant or even a wild turkey, but she was satisfied with the prairie chicken. I'm not sure whether Christmas dinner came flying through the window as a result of God's blessing us with manna from heaven or His cursing the prairie chicken with poor eyesight and a bad sense of direction. In any case, there was fowl for dinner. The prairie chicken was delicious, too, especially after you scraped off the burnt part.

HOT LUNCH

*M*om cooked the noon hot lunch at the Squaw Valley school. These meals were probably the strangest in the entire history of hot-lunch programs. It wasn't that my mother didn't know how to cook. In fact, she could turn out a delicious meal whenever the mood struck her, which was about once every four or five years. Normally, however, she had absolutely no interest in the preparation of food. Cooking was a nuisance to her, serving no other purpose than to ease the pangs of hunger. Surely, her hot lunches would have been anticipated by her pupils with unease, and even dread, had it not been that they were cloaked in suspense and mystery. Because blizzards locked up the valley for weeks and months at a time during winter, some agency trucked in cans of food for the hot-lunch program during the fall. I can't remember where this food was stored at the school, but wherever it was, the place leaked. All the labels became soaked and came off the cans. Because there was no refrigeration, when you opened a can, you ate the ingredients, no matter what. This is what led to the suspense and mystery in our hot-lunch program. When the noon hour came, Mom would select a couple of the large cans from storage. Slowly, savoring the suspense, she would begin cranking the can opener as her students leaned forward at their desks, wondering what treat lay in store for them this day.

"Well, plums," Mom would say, staring into the can. "Yes, I think it's plums. It looks like plums and smells like plums so it must be plums." Then she would open the second can, for we had two-can hot lunches. "Prunes," she would say. "It looks as if we're going to have plums and prunes today. Doesn't that sound good!" She would then slop the plums and prunes into a big pot on the barrel stove, and we students would sit there glumly awaiting hot lunch. My mother loved to gamble, and I think opening the unlabeled cans appealed to her sense of chance. It was like drawing to an inside straight.

The hot-lunch supplies also included bags of rice and cornmeal, which got a little weevily toward the end of winter. Even now I regard a raisin in a bowl of rice with suspicion. I like my rice pure white, with no little dark things roaming about in it. Mom seldom bothered with the rice or cornmeal, not because of the weevils but because it required too much preparation. Every cloud has a silver lining. Fortunately, the neighbors and school parents contributed to the hot lunches—potatoes, onions, carrots, eggs, milk, home-baked bread, and whatever other surplus food they might have on hand. In the spring we would collect wild mushrooms, and Mom would fry them up with scrambled eggs for lunch. They were delicious, after you scraped off the burnt part. Occasionally, someone would anonymously drop off a hindquarter of deer at the door of the school. Ours was one of the few hot-lunch programs in the country to serve wild mushrooms and poached venison.

A DILEMMA

*M*y father became increasingly ill our first year at Squaw Valley, and it soon became apparent even to me that he was dying. He visited us only occasionally at the school, would stay a few days or a week, and then be gone again. One day Mom said she had to take him to a hospital in Boise and that my sister and I would have to stay with a family that lived back in the mountains. It was a sad and miserable time, because I knew I would never see my dad again. Now I had to go live with some strangers, the Whipples. As it turned out, the Whipples were a nice, fat old couple, and staying with them wasn't too bad. The one problem was that Mrs. Whipple insisted that I sleep in the same bed with her. To complicate matters, the Whipples' privy was a good fifty yards away from the house during the day and in excess of a mile at night. I tried to avoid making any journeys to it after dark. So one night I woke up having to go to the bathroom real bad. I climbed over the great snoring mound that was Mrs. Whipple, scrubbed a hole in the frost of the window, and stared out at the distant privy, which had gusts of snow whipping around the outside. Just as I suspected, I could make out the dark outline of an ax murderer waiting for me inside. Forget that! I crawled around on the frigid floor and felt under the bed for a chamber pot. No luck. I shook Mrs. Whipple's shoulder, but she continued to snore blissfully on, undisturbed. The cold floor was numbing my bare feet as I danced up and down, growing ever more desperate. It then occurred to me that there was only one thing to do: pee on the floor! But wait. If I did that, it would freeze to ice by morning. Mrs. Whipple would lumber out of bed, slip on the puddle of frozen piddle, and possibly break a leg or an arm. Even if she didn't seriously injure herself, she might regard my peeing on her floor as a lapse of good manners. I decided my only practical, safe, and decent option was to climb back under the covers and deliberately wet the bed. Deliberately wetting a bed is much harder than you might suppose, but I accomplished it, and went back to sleep. Bed-wetting could at least be passed off as a neurosis of some kind and would never be interpreted as bad manners. Strangely, Mrs. Whipple never mentioned the bed-wetting to me, but she did to my mother. I explained the situation to Mom, about how I had saved Mrs. Whipple from a nasty fall, maybe even a broken leg or arm. "Sounds reasonable to me," Mom said. She was a person who understood the importance of acting with cold logic in desperate situations.

CRAZY PEOPLE

An old woodcutter lived on the mountain behind the school at Squaw Valley. He was regarded by most of the community as quite mad, and probably dangerously so. Even though the Old Woodcutter, as he was known, struck terror into the hearts of most people in the community, my father liked him and would often invite him in for a cup of coffee. He was gnarled and hunchbacked, with a scraggly beard, long white hair, and wild, darting eyes, all of which features were ominously complemented by a double-bitted ax he routinely carried over his shoulder. (In recalling the practical joke my father played on them with the Ouija board, both Buck and Wally said later that it wasn't so much a spook they worried about encountering at the big tree as the Old Woodcutter. The ax murderer I detected in Mrs. Whipple's privy the night I saved her from a broken leg also greatly resembled the Old Woodcutter.) The odd thing was that when Dad invited him in for coffee, the Old Woodcutter always parked his ax and most of his insanity

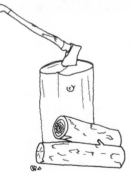

at the door. Dad knew his real name, too—Bill, I think—and always referred to him by it. He and Bill would sit by the old barrel stove and tell each other stories, laughing uproariously. I even recall one of Bill's stories. One time he was on a battleship and an enemy fighter plane was zooming right at him and Bill dived over the side of the battleship, swam underneath it, and came up the other side, and you should have seen the look on that enemy pilot's face. Bill and Dad laughed and laughed at that story. After Bill had left, the Troll said to Dad, "Don't you think Bill is a little bit off?"

"Crazy as hell," Dad said. "Don't you listen to his stories? He's not a bad sort, though. Really quite a likable old codger."

Many years later I happened to run into a man who knew my dad, and he told me that my father was one of the kindest and most generous men he had ever known. I think that must have been true.

My mother wasn't much bothered by insanity either. She seemed to have no fear of the Old Woodcutter, and even bought wood from him. She would have him in for a cup of coffee from time to time after my father died. She was more afraid of being bored to death by his stories than being murdered with his ax. It is probable that old Bill was responsible for the poached venison left outside our door from time to time, maybe as a token of his friendship for my father.

I witnessed my mother deal with insanity on two remarkable occasions simply by ignoring it. One day years later, while I was home from college, she took me with her to visit an old friend of hers who had been committed to an asylum. I was startled and shocked by the sights, sounds, and smells of the place, but Mom strode on ahead of me as if totally unaware of the surroundings. Maybe she viewed the world as totally insane anyway, and the asylum therefore was not much different from the norm, except more concentrated. We found her friend, Sadie, crouched on a cot, half-naked, filthy, her hair a ferocious tangle and her eyes staring vacantly into space. She showed not the slightest indication of recognizing us or even being aware of our presence.

"Hi, Sadie," Mom said, pulling up a chair and lighting a cigarette. "Guess what? You're not going to believe this, but you know that mean Mrs. Cronckle who used to live behind you, the one with all those snotty little kids. Well . . ." And Mom went on to tell the latest gossip. Pretty soon Sadie's eyes began to slip into focus. She came out of her crouch and moved across the bed toward my mother, pulling her gown up around her shoulders. A faint smile formed on her lips. "Mabel, give me a cigarette," she said. And pretty soon they were sitting there talking, laughing, and smoking, just like it was old times. Gossip had momentarily overpowered insanity.

"What a terrible place!" I said to Mom after we had left. "I can't believe such places still exist."

"What place?" she said. "What are you talking about?"

Mom had been oblivious to the whole dreadful experience. Either that or she knew terrible places when she saw them, and this one didn't come anywhere near meeting the criteria.

One summer morning at The Place, we heard someone screaming outside and got up to look out the kitchen window. A huge madman was standing out in the yard, waving a little tattered magazine in the air, and yelling at the house. He was taller than anyone we had ever seen and wore a dirty black coat that reached almost to his ankles. His gray hair swirled wildly in the wind, and his face was twisted in rage. He was a fearsome sight.

"Good lord, what now!" Mom said angrily. "Can't a person have a cup of coffee in peace anymore!"

She then stomped out of the house and confronted the madman, who seemed nearly twice her height. My sister and I (then about sixteen and ten) watched from the kitchen window as the madman tore a page out of the little magazine and thrust it at Mom. She glanced at it, then thrust it back at the madman. Then she pointed in the direction of the nearest property line, her lips moving angrily. She turned and stormed back into the house.

"Can you believe it?" she said to us. "That fool tried to sell me a page out of an old *Reader's Digest* for ten cents! I could buy the whole damn magazine for fifteen cents, and a new one besides! The man must be crazy to think I'd fall for something like that." She refilled her coffee cup and plopped angrily down into a chair.

The Troll and I continued to watch the madman out the window. He stood silently in the yard for a few moments, his arms hanging down at his sides, the magazine in one hand, the torn page in the other. After a bit, he wandered off dejectedly toward the next farm. Later, we learned that tough, hard farmers all up and down the road had bought pages of the magazine for ten cents each from the madman, and considered them a bargain. The man may have been crazy, but he was a pretty fair salesman.

We had our local crazy people, too, but they were for the most part friendly and decent folk. One insane old couple lived not far from our house. Sometimes they would pass through our yard in the middle of the night, raving madly at each other. "It's just the poor old Bedlams," Mom would tell my sister and me. "Go back to sleep."

Mrs. Bedlam offered my sister a glass of cider one day, and as the Troll thirstily guzzled the last drop, her hostess asked how she liked it. "It's good," the Troll said, smacking her lips.

"I think so, too," said Mrs. Bedlam. "And the mice love it. Every morning I have to dip a couple of their little drowned bodies out of the vat. How about another glassful, dear?"

My father once made the mistake of accepting a glass of lemonade from Mrs. Bedlam.

"How do you get this nice green color?" he asked, thinking the worst.

"Oh, I just add a bit of Herbert's after-shave lotion," Mrs. Bedlam replied. "Makes it pretty, don't you think?"

"Quite tangy, too," Dad said, and drank down the lemonade. Anyone who can mistake steamboat fuel for candy isn't going to mind a bit of after-shave lotion in his lemonade.

When she was a troll of six or seven, Patricia, to spice up the conversation, told the Bedlams that there had just been a terrible bus accident on the highway near our place. Dozens of people had been injured and she didn't know how many had been killed outright. The Bedlams grabbed blankets and bandages and rushed off to aid the survivors. The poor old couple actually believed something my sister told them, that's how crazy they were.

FAREWELL, FREEDOM!

My sister cannot dredge up a single fond memory of the two years we lived at Squaw Valley. Perhaps it is because she was a troll of twelve and thirteen instead of a boy of six and seven. For me, they were years of almost undiluted pleasure. Half a century later, I can still return to that time and place and treat my senses to the exact sights, sounds, smells, tastes, and textures once enjoyed by that strange little boy I am reported to have been.

It is night, and I am lying on my cot in the back of the schoolroom watching the light show on the ceiling and log walls, a light show produced by the hundreds of holes in the rusted-out old barrel stove. I smell the chalk dust and pencil shavings, woodsmoke, kerosene, rotting wood, moldy apples, rancid flour and cornmeal, burnt food. I hear the brush of snow against the frosted windowpanes, the ominous creaking of the ceiling timbers, the tinny rumble of wood chunks settling in the stove, the whine and sizzle of a blizzard outside, and the thrilling, chilling howls of the valley's wolf pack as it swings over the ridge above the school. I go to sleep and dream of spring, of the white trilliums popping up behind the receding snow, the morel mushrooms exploding from the ground, the slimy clusters of frogs' eggs floating in the swamp, trout flashing in the log-tangled pools of Goose Creek, mallard couples setting up housekeeping in the brushy, flooded meadows, and everywhere the great all-enveloping wetness of April.

By the spring of 1941, I could read quite well and pretty much divided my time between reading and exploring on Goose Creek, a place of endless surprise and fascination to me, not to mention a few dunkings. Indeed, had it not been for reading, and my fear of the dark, I might have run totally wild. There is evidence that I came close. I recall scrambling up the muddy creek bank one day near the end of the school year to find all the regular pupils lined up as if they were about to be shot by a firing squad. They were all slicked up in their good pants and shirts and dresses, with their faces washed and their hair combed. A strange man with a black hood over his head, the executioner no doubt, was bent over some sort of contraption. I backed off to watch. This could be good! Suddenly, it occurred to me that the man was taking the school picture and I was about to be left out. I rushed over and got in line next to Barbara, the only other second grader, just as the picture was snapped. Many years later, I came across the picture in a photo album belonging to one of the students. The line of youngsters diminished in size from the eighth graders down to the second graders, everyone combed and cleaned and neatly attired, except for the strange small creature at the very end. His long hair is wild, his face dirty, his shirt torn, and his bib overalls, hanging by one strap, are caked with mud, and he is beaming with the happy assurance that he is going to turn out looking absolutely terrific in the photograph. And, I must say, he did.

"Cripes, Mom," I said after the photo was taken, "I almost missed being in the school picture!"

"Yes," she said.

I then rushed back to the creek.

Unbeknownst to me, my life of freedom and adventure at Squaw Valley was rapidly drawing to an end. My mother had been hired to teach arithmetic in the junior high school at Sandpoint. I was shocked and outraged when Mom broke the news to me. Had she gone mad? How could she even think of leaving all this behind?

"Well," I said sullenly, "I guess I'll have to go to third grade at Farmin School."

"No," she said.

"No?" I said, brightening.

"Second grade."

Second grade! Again! My own mother had flunked me! The charge was too many absences. I thought that had to be some kind of achievement, considering that I lived in the schoolroom.

Even now I shudder at recalling my first day back at Farmin School, particularly the eerie sound of the second-grade door clanking shut behind me.

My second-grade classmates were still reading about Dick and Jane and Spot, the stupidest and most boring dog ever to scratch at the door of literature. They had never even heard of my heroes, Huck Finn and Tom Sawyer. Well, I knew one thing. The second grade hadn't been built yet that could hold me.

SCHOOL

During my seven-year term at Farmin School, second grade through eighth, I was a model prisoner. One of my classmates says she remembers me as being shy and quiet. I remember her as being a grapefruit. Odd the tricks memory plays on one. The fact is, I was rather dashing and debonair, a small Rhett Butler without the mustache. It's hard for me to believe that the grapefruit didn't notice.

At that time, families pretty much stayed put, and so you moved along through the grades year after year with the same cell mates. I can still remember them distinctly: Marilyn, Bob, Ruthie, Eugene, Lester, Earl, Loretta Jean, Ewing, Pansy Ray, Polly, Jake, Melvin, Johnnie, La Rue, Dick, Ila, Donna, Clyde, Merl, Richard, Robert, Margaret, Bill, Paul, Teddy, Darrell, Eddie, Gordon, Betty, Geraldine, Elinore, Jackie, Leroy, and, of course, Pat. Some went and some came, but the class as a whole retained a distinct identity, of which each of us was a part. For the first time I began to feel that I belonged to something larger than myself. It was terrible.

Over the years we members of the Class of 1952 shared a common history of the classroom and bits and pieces of one another's private lives. The winter we were in third grade, Melvin trapped a skunk in a box and had some trouble removing it. The third-grade windows were left wide open his first day back in class, and finally the teacher sent him to study with the janitor for the rest of the week. In fourth grade, Bill showed me what it feels like to get kneed in the groin, as a scientific experiment, and Eugene and I floated our first raft down Sand Creek. In fifth grade, Ila and Eugene and I nearly got caught by a train crossing a railroad trestle. In sixth grade, Jake and I almost got caught swimming naked in the creek by a bunch of girls and had to hide in a nettle patch, and Eddie and I almost got caught by a bull while fishing. (We were always almost getting caught by something in those days.) Lester started me collecting stamps, which resulted in several mail-order stamp companies threatening to send a team of assassins after me if I didn't pay for all the stamps they had sent me unrequested. (I thought they were gifts.) Ewing and I organized the Crescent Boys' Club, which had a membership of two and dissolved when we each got one vote in the election for president. Dick usually fainted during school inoculations, this entertainment distracting us from the awaiting needles. Margaret was the best singer. I was the worst. (In sixth grade, I practiced my song for at least a month, and several students and even the music teacher, Mrs. Seniff, said they almost recognized the tune.) Richard, when his schedule allowed, practiced his beating-up technique on me after school. One day I recruited Leroy to help me beat up Richard, and afterward Richard said he was sorry—sorry he hadn't thought before of beating up two guys at once, because it was so much more fun. Ruthie was my girlfriend for a while, even though we never went anywhere together. She gave me a *Big Little Book* for Christmas, and I gave her a nice bar of soap, which pretty well ended our relationship. In seventh grade, we drew names for an exchange of presents at Christmas, and Merl gave Richard a model airplane, and Richard was so insulted to be given a toy for Christmas that Merl had to hide after school to keep from getting beaten up. The following summer, Merl and I were fishing on a mountain creek and saw a fully loaded logging truck come rocking and swaying down a steep and dangerous road. Richard was driving the truck. He probably had to sit on a pillow to see over the dashboard. I then beat up Merl for giving Richard a toy for Christmas. That was the summer that the guys at the bakery threw a big pot of grease at Merl and me, and Merl, watching the grease descending, ran full tilt into a parked car and knocked himself cold, and then the grease landed on him. The winter of seventh grade, a tough kid I'd never seen before punched me in the face and knocked me flat on my back into a ditch full of ice water. Oh, those were the days, my friend.

Thusly was the identity of our class knit into the rich, colorful, and distinctive fabric of my memory, now somewhat frayed and faded but still unraveled. Looking back now, eroded as I am by time and chaos, I must in all honesty confess that I didn't really dislike school—I detested it.

Now that I didn't live in the schoolroom, I could feign fatal illnesses and stay home whenever I felt the urge, which was often. Then my grandmother came to live with us. Gram had a home remedy for childhood illnesses that never failed to work. The ingredients were secret, but I know they included sulfur, balsam-fir sap, and probably an eye of newt, a toe of frog, some wool of bat, and tongue of dog, with a dash of blindworm's sting thrown in. A teaspoonful of the stuff would send you into a violent fit of gagging. "I'm cured! I'm cured!" you would shout between gags. Then Gram said that just smelling and looking at the remedy wouldn't cure a person— you actually had to *swallow* it! I suspected you could approach a dead hog with a spoonful of the remedy and the animal would leap up and go to school and probably get fairly decent grades, if it hadn't been dead too long.

Because we seldom had fresh fruit or vegetables during those early years, my mother feared we might come down with scurvy. Consequently, my life was blighted by another evil: cod-liver oil. Every morning I had to take a spoonful of the ghastly stuff. "Stop that bellowing and take your oil," Gram would order. "It'll put hair on your chest." She was right, too. I was the only eight-year-old in school with hair on his chest. One thing about having to take cod-liver oil first thing in the morning, all the rest of the day was easy living by comparison.

During the winter, school mornings at our house resembled something out of Dante's *Inferno*. Because our house was heated by a wood stove, which would usually go out during the night,

and because my mother hadn't known about insulation when she had the house built, ice would form on the north inside walls, some winters up to a depth of an inch or two. It looked as if we had a frozen waterfall inside the house. Blizzards would drift snow up to the eaves. As the cold increased day after day, our lives moved in increasingly smaller orbits around the stoves, the cooking one in the kitchen and the heating one in the living room. We slept without heat in the bedrooms, under a great weight of blankets and quilts, and were warm enough in bed. But we awoke to an icy nightmare.

Mom got up first to build the fire in the kitchen stove. Several years later, after she had remarried, my stepfather insisted upon building the morning fire. But until then, Mom handled the chore herself. The procedure was this: She would stick a hand out from under the bedcovers and in the same motion shut off the alarm and grope blindly for her pack of Camels. She would lie there in bed, smoking her cigarette, like a soldier in trench warfare preparing himself mentally to go over the top and charge the enemy with fixed bayonet. I suppose she realized the dangers of smoking in bed, but getting burnt up probably seemed minor compared with what lay ahead. Then she would spring from the covers, dive into her coat and boots, stalk out to the kitchen, cram some firewood and kindling into the stove, douse it copiously with kerosene, and toss a lighted match at it—*kaaaBLOOOOSH!* The stove would then do its impression of a malfunctioning flamethrower, with fire and smoke squirting from every orifice. It was a frightening thing to witness. That is why my stepfather later insisted on building the fire himself.

Mom would next put the coffee on to boil, and while every last atom of caffeine and acid was being rendered from the grounds, she would sit down at the kitchen table and have another cigarette. This is one image of my mother inscribed indelibly in my mind: She is sitting there at the kitchen table in her coat, nightgown showing around the edges, her feet in boots. She is slumped slightly forward against the table and the cold, with a cigarette dangling from her lips. Her eyes are hard and as sharp and frigid as icicles. Her silence is stony and ominous. She is marshaling her resources, preparing to ride against the Furies. This is not a good time to disturb her with such a ridiculous question as "What's for breakfast?" Her plan of action and cigarette both finished, suddenly, miraculously, she is transformed. She is on her feet, joking, laughing, snapping out orders—do this, do that, get a move on. Her cheerfulness is terrible and incomprehensible. The Furies still await.

During blizzards, when the road from the house to the highway was blocked with drifts, Mom, the Troll, and I all rode the school bus to school. We would get up at five, hover around the stove until breakfast was ready—"I guess we'll have milk toast this morning, doesn't that sound good?"— and then prepare for the hike to the highway. Since it was dark and we didn't own a flashlight, Mom would make a torch, wrapping a section of broom handle with rags, which she would douse with kerosene. Then we would go out the door single file and Mom would ignite her torch. The Troll and I would tramp glumly along behind her as she picked out the trail, the flames of the torch leaping savagely about in the wind and sending our grotesque shadows dancing hideously against the drifts of snow. I can remember thinking on one such occasion, All this misery, and for what? Just to get to school.

The worst morning I recall—there were many close competitors for worst—happened as a result of Mom's preference for hiring criminals and madmen to do work around the place. The madman who installed the water-heating coils in the wood stove made a predictable error in the installation, and one winter morning the coil exploded, sending stove lids ricocheting about the kitchen. Boiling water and steam shot out and scalded Mom on the arm, badly enough that after teaching school for the day she had to have it treated by a doctor. The mention of criminals reminds me of the time one named Shorty tried to extort extra money from Mom for a little job he had performed. Mom refused to pay, naturally. Then Shorty, the fool, tried to intimidate my mother. "I'll get you for this!" he shouted, shaking his fist at her.

"We'll see about that," Mom told him. "If you ever set foot on this place again, I'll shoot you."

I considered this an empty threat, because we didn't even own a gun at the time. But that evening Mom came home with a .32-caliber automatic. I figured that if Shorty was as big a fool as I thought, he was also a dead man. Luckily for him, he had enough sense never to set foot on our place again.

When the roads were merely exceedingly dangerous but not impassable, Mom drove our own car to school. There she would stand early morning duty as playground supervisor, teach three classes of arithmetic, stand playground duty for the noon hour, teach three more classes, and then drive home to a cold house and the evening chore of correcting a hundred or so arithmetic papers. She considered this living high on the hog.

In the evening, the three of us would drive home in the dark, the Troll and I starving and wondering what awaited us for dinner. Looking back, I now realize that my mother was a highly imaginative cook. "What's for supper, Mom?" I would ask. She would frown for a moment, the thought of preparing supper not having occurred to her. Then she would brighten and say cheerfully, "I know! We'll have milk toast!

Doesn't that sound good?" The Troll and I would stare at her in disbelief and horror. But here is where Mom engaged her imagination for cooking. "What we'll do," she'd say enthusiastically, "is we'll cut some nice thick slices of homemade bread. Then we'll toast the slices to a rich golden brown and spread them with fresh butter. We'll heat the milk nice and hot and sprinkle in a little salt and lots of good pepper and pour the milk over the toast. Yummm!" By the time she was done talking, you would think milk toast was the gourmet treat of your life, and you couldn't wait to get home and dive into it. The milk toast was usually pretty good, too, after you scraped off the burnt part.

Milk toast was my mother's favorite dish. Once when I was in college, I invited a girlfriend home for dinner. "What's for dinner, Mom?" I asked.

"Milk toast," Mom said. "Doesn't that sound good?"

My girlfriend loved the milk toast. So I married her.

I don't remember much about my thousands of hours in Farmin School classrooms. Most of the teachers were very good. One or two were crazy or vicious, and at least one was sadistic. None was dumb. In those days, there weren't so many career opportunities for smart and independent women, so the brightest seemed to go into teaching. We learned our lessons whether we wanted to or not, even from the occasional crazy, vicious, or sadistic teacher. In fact, we probably learned more from the vicious teacher. A little fear is a great motivator when it comes to learning something you don't want to learn. We had our share of dumb kids, but I doubt a single one of them made it through school without learning to read, write, and do arithmetic, although you probably wouldn't pick any of them to be on your Trivial Pursuit team. Many of the students in my class went on to distinguished careers in the professions. A few students at the school became bums and criminals, of course, but at least they weren't illiterate bums and criminals. Because there was no such thing as "social promotion" in those years, some of the dumbest kids were like particles of water in a wave. They rose and fell in the waves of successive classes, but after a wave had passed, they were still in the same place. One friend of mine was practically shaving by the time he got out of fourth grade. The best and nicest teacher was Mrs. Hickey, who taught sixth grade. I met her again not too long ago, and she said that even after forty some years she could remember me in her class, right down to the desk I sat at. I don't know whether that is good or not. I certainly didn't distinguish myself as a scholar, so I must have impressed her some other way. Maybe it was because I was dashing and debonair, like a short Rhett Butler.

I was academically consistent, however. On a graph, my grades would form a straight line at the C level, with regular dips for my D in music. From first to eighth grade, I cannot recall a single subject in school that interested me even for a second, although there probably were some. When we reached junior high, we were segregated into three classes according to intelligence: smart, average, and dumb. I was in the average group. If you obtained a B average over a report-card period, you were supposed to be promoted to the smart class. For some reason obscure to me now, possibly because of a smart girl I was interested in, I actually studied with some diligence for one six-week period and achieved all A's and B's. My grade points exceeded the number required to be promoted to the smart class. But I wasn't promoted. The principal, who was in charge of such promotions, considered my grades a temporary aberration of some sort, possibly due to a rare alignment of the planets. And he was right. By the time my next report card came out, the planets had realigned themselves to a C average.

Not all kids in the dumb division were dumb. I remember one boy who looked dumb, acted dumb, and got dumb grades. When he took the intelligence test to join the Navy, however, he achieved the highest score ever in the inland Pacific Northwest region. I think he became an admiral, although not right away.

How did I survive the iron tyranny of school? There is only one answer. Every classroom at Farmin School looked out on beautiful ranges of mountains, either the Selkirks or the Cabinets. I would sit at my desk and stare off at those mountains and hear them whispering to me: "Come. We are waiting for you. Come." I daydreamed of going up into the mountains to live. During spelling, I cut down trees and notched the logs for a cabin. I put up the walls during geography. I split cedar shakes and roofed the cabin with them during arithmetic. I shot a deer and turned it into smoked jerky during history. During English, I relaxed from my labors and sauntered down to a tumbling stream to catch a couple of trout for supper. Suddenly, I was attacked! Not by a grizzly bear or a mountain lion but by the deadly dangling participle, the insidious infinitive, and the ghastly gerund. "Patrick!" the teacher snapped. "If I may interrupt your reverie for a moment, would you please name the three kinds of verbals?"

MOUNTAINS

*I*t is difficult to convey what mountains meant to me. They were freedom, adventure, and mystery, and something else, something bordering almost on the spiritual. I wanted somehow to possess the mountains. For many years, I tried painting pictures of them, but that didn't work particularly well. Later, I wrote about them, and that was a bit better, but something less than satisfying. Now I know that you can't possess mountains. They possess you.

Jackie Kennedy (not Mrs. Onassis, by the way) and I climbed to the top of the mountain behind my home when we were eight years old, because some strange force made us do it. As we neared the summit, we ran into snow. In some places, we sank in up to our hips in the melting drifts. Both of us were half crying from pain and exhaustion. Still, we climbed and climbed, and at last reached the highest peak. We stood there in the chill wind, savoring the scenery and our triumph. Off to the south lay the toy town of Sandpoint, and spreading out from it, the majestic, deep-blue expanse of Lake Pend Oreille. To the north, east, and west lay endless waves of mountains, whitecapped with snow and ragged with granite peaks. Immediately below us lay the patchwork of little farms and woodlots, with the brushy line of Sand Creek meandering to town. It was all pretty darn nice.

On our way back down the mountain, Jackie slipped on some ice and shot off over the lip of a cliff. I climbed down and found his body wedged between two large rocks. I thought he was dead. By then, I could recognize a dilemma when I saw one. If I stayed with him, I would freeze in the deepening cold of fast-approaching night. If I left him, the wolves and coyotes might eat him. I decided the only practical thing to do was bury him. Fortunately for Jackie, he started to regain consciousness before I had piled more than half a dozen rocks on his body. He survived the fall with nothing more serious than a few broken ribs, but also the wisdom that it was not a good idea to get knocked unconscious around me.

Oddly enough, I was later suspected of burying another one of my friends. Vern Schulze stopped by my house one day and told me he was running away from home. I said I thought that was a great idea and wished I had thought of it myself. I didn't have anything else to do that day, so I decided to run away with him, at least until it got dark. While we were running away, I cut myself on some barbed wire and used my shirt to sop up the blood. Then I stuffed my shirt down a hollow stump, for no particular reason, except I thought that was what Tom Sawyer would do with a bloody shirt. Late in the afternoon, I got tired of running away and went home. Because Vern had never before disappeared for more than a few hours, his parents became worried and organized a search party to look for him. (I could have been missing for days before my mother noticed.) I told the searchers I hadn't laid eyes on Vern all week. No one believed me, but I stuck to my story. Then the searchers found my bloody shirt in the hollow stump and instantly recognized it as mine, since the few shirts I owned could easily be identified as mine by anyone in the county. They were almost like a set of fingerprints. So the searchers, unable to think of any reason why I would try to hide a bloody shirt, leaped to the conclusion that Vern had been killed in a fall from a horse or a cow, and I had buried him, after wiping up his blood with my shirt. Such was my reputation in those days. Vern gave up running away and returned home on his own. This happened shortly after nightfall, which he said was just a coincidence, and he hoped no one would attach undue significance to it.

That night Mom asked me what I had been up to all day.

"I ran away," I said.

"That's nice," she said. "Now eat your milk toast before it curdles."

My mother was not what you would call an overprotective parent. She also knew that my fear of the dark was like a giant bow that would shoot me home shortly after the sun went down.

Day trips into the high country were fine, but I knew I would never succeed as a mountain man until I conquered my fear of the dark. It was simply too impractical for a mountain man to commute. ("Any sign of beaver a half-day's ride from the fort?") From a very young age, six or seven, I tried to cure myself of this embarrassing weakness in my character. It was something my mother absolutely could not comprehend—fear of the dark, fear of anything for that matter. The Troll, on the other hand, understood my weakness all too well, and exploited it to the utmost. She would wait for hours in a darkened room, waiting for my hand to come in, groping blindly for the light switch. Then she would grab my hand. On one such occasion, I gave her severe whiplash from snapping her about in the air, trying to get the awful thing to let go. "Would you shut up that screeching and leave your sister alone!" Mom bellowed.

When we were in fifth grade, Eugene and I tried to sleep

out down by the creek one night. Eugene was not afraid of the dark and possibly had never encountered anyone who was. Little did he realize his companion was a victim of this dreadful malady. Eugene lay there in his sleeping bag, staring blissfully up at the dark and chatting calmly away.

"Polly sure is pretty, ain't she?" he said.

"Um," I replied.

"Ila's almost as pretty, don't you think?"

"Um."

"Which one would you like for a girlfriend?"

"Um."

I could feel my whole body winding itself up into a giant spring. I tried to think of some excuse as to why I was shortly to depart for home, but fear had overloaded the circuits of my brain. In a flash, without so much as a good-bye to Eugene, I was out of my sleeping bag and streaking for home. Eugene passed me before I had cleared the top of the creek bank. His head was twisted around backward like an owl's, as he tried to catch sight of what he assumed must be in hot pursuit of us.

"Wh-what was it?" he asked later.

"A bear," I said, "I think it was a bear."

By the time I was eleven, I still hadn't managed to sleep out a single night. I tried again and again, but each time the bow of darkness would shoot me into the house. Some of the shots covered a considerable distance. Once Vern Schulze and I tried to sleep out in the woods behind his place. About midnight, I discovered myself flying across the field in front of my own house. I had traveled over half a mile and crossed four barbed-wire fences, two ditches, numerous logs, and a highway without noticing any of them. Vern's folks couldn't recall ever having seen a grizzly in their woods before, and took a great deal of interest in my report of the sighting. They said they thought I had probably mistaken a black bear for a grizzly, which was understandable. "After all, it was pretty dark."

"Right," I said.

Shortly after my twelfth birthday I realized that if I was ever to become a mountain man, I had to overcome my fear of the dark and sleep out for one entire night. I also knew that the only way to do this was to sleep out so far away I couldn't possibly run home. So I organized my first camping trip, recruiting my friends Vern, Kenny Thompson, and Norm Nelson for the expedition. That trip was one of the great educational experiences of my life. It was kid camping's finest hour.

Our intended campsite was approximately a three-mile hike from Vern's house—two miles across farmland and another mile up Schweitzer Creek, a tiny stream tumbling out of the mountains and flowing through tangled logjams, thick forest, devil's clubs, huge rocks, sheer cliffs, and assorted beaver dams. In other words, the ideal place for a first camping trip. It would be impossible to run home over such terrain in the dark of night.

This being our first camping trip, we took only the essentials, namely everything we owned, with the exception of a few clothes and our bicycles. Our packs weighed in at over four hundred pounds apiece and contained roughly the following: three hatchets, one ax, two machetes, a cast-iron skillet, assorted pots and pans, knives, forks, and spoons, a canvas tarp, a mountain tent, a jungle hammock, four war-surplus chicken-down sleeping bags, extra sets of clothes, a first-aid kit, cameras, binoculars, fishing rods and tackle, cans of worms, jars of grasshoppers, and our grub—a dozen boiled eggs, a dozen raw eggs, a slab of bacon, five pounds of potatoes, three onions, several quart jars of canned fruit, a box of cornflakes, milk for the cornflakes, a pound of wieners, buns for the wieners, two bags of potato chips, three cans of pork 'n' beans, two loaves of bread, a dozen cinnamon rolls, marshmallows, and assorted candy bars. There was more, much more, but that is all I can remember.

Before our departure, we spread our camp gear and grub out on the Schulzes' lawn for a final inventory. Vern's dad,

Frank, came out and surveyed the scene: "You boys sure you've got enough stuff?" he said. "Remember, you're going to be gone for two nights." That caused us some anxiety, but we figured we could live off the land if we ran out of food.

Our packs were so heavy we had taken two rest breaks by the time we were out of the Schulzes' yard. The longest three miles of our lives lay ahead. I would lift one of my feet and then have to lean forward and shift the weight of the pack forward to get the foot back on the ground and complete the step. Somehow, hours later, we made it to our campsite, a small gravelly beach next to a tiny waterfall, with a rock overhang to shelter us from any rain. When we finally dropped our packs, the earth settled several inches beneath our feet and we moved about with long floating strides, in the manner of astronauts on the moon two decades later.

A strange thing happened that night. We had just climbed into our sleeping bags and my old enemy, darkness, had closed in around us. It was the darkest darkness I had ever experienced, but I was so exhausted from packing in that I couldn't have cared less. The hard ground felt like a featherbed, the rocks under my head like freshly fluffed pillows. Just as I was floating off into oblivion, I heard a frantic rustling. With great effort, I raised my three-pound eyelids. Norm was out of his sleeping bag and stuffing it into his pack. He crammed his other gear in on top of it, shouldered the pack, and shot like an arrow off into the dark toward home.

"What's Norm doing?" Kenny asked wearily.

"Going home, I guess," Vern said.

"I wonder how come," Kenny said.

"I don't know," Vern said.

Apparently, they hadn't heard that old familiar twang of the bow of darkness. I drifted happily off to sleep. I was about to pass the qualifying exam for becoming a mountain man.

The next morning Kenny, Vern, and I ate twenty-eight crisp-fried trout for breakfast, but they were small. We also had fried potatoes and onions, pancakes with homemade

maple syrup, and bacon flambé, which we doused with a
bucket of water. We made cowboy coffee by tossing a couple
or three handfuls of coffee into a pot of boiling water, and
called it good. We hadn't marked the boiled eggs but had no
difficulty distinguishing them from the raw
eggs, because the raw eggs were all puddled
up in the bottom of a pack. When we needed
beaten eggs for pancakes or biscuits, we simply squeezed some out of an extra pair of
socks or underwear from the bottom of the
pack. This was a camping tip I later passed
on to other kid campers. We divided our
time between fishing for more trout for our
next breakfast, cooking, and eating. That's what you do on a
kid camping trip: fish cook eat fish cook eat fish cook eat.

We had three memorable scares the second night, about
the right number for a successful camping trip. When we
returned from fishing that evening, a breeze had come up, and
the canyon was almost dark. We were startled to see a huge,
batlike creature prowling about our camp, gobbling up our
grub. We stood at a distance and threw rocks at the beast,
but it ignored us and continued its rampage. Cautiously, we
moved closer, and discovered that we had been trying to drive
my mountain tent out of camp by throwing rocks at it. Fortunately, the mountain tent had eaten very little of our food
supply, which was already seriously depleted. We thought we
might have to ration ourselves to six full meals a day and
snacks.

We didn't bother to use the mountain tent that night, pre-
ferring to sleep out under the dark. We had discovered some
bear signs not far from camp that day, and were now a bit
nervous. Our finely tuned ears picked up every nuance of
sound—the distant whistle of a train, the hum of a mosquito,
the snap and pop of our campfire's dying embers, the watery
clicks and rattles of stones disturbed by the rushing creek, and
the pitter-patter of ants rushing to and from our grub pile.

While the rest of our bodies dozed fitfully, our ears stood sentry duty. Sometime during the night, we were awakened by a terrible racket right in camp. The sentries cried, "Bear!" We lay deathly still, rolling only our eyeballs in the direction of the racket, now partially drowned out by the frantic drumming of three hearts. We could make out a large, dark shape in the vicinity of the noise. I stared so hard at the shape my optic nerves cramped up. Aha! The black shape was a stump that had been in camp all along. My eyeballs scoped down to the source of the racket—a bag of potato chips! A chipmunk stuck his head out of the bag to check on the three kid campers. Satisfied that he had killed us with fright, he went back into the bag. Forever afterward, I would regard chipmunks with suspicion, now that I knew how deadly they could be.

Vern and I slept through the third fright of the night. Toward morning, Kenny awoke and looked across the creek, which was only about six feet wide. A huge black bear padded silently up along the other side of the creek as Kenny watched. The bear didn't so much as glance in our direction. Kenny then went calmly back to sleep, or so he claimed. The next morning Vern and I investigated and found the bear's tracks, just to check on Kenny's story. We also found a couple of scorch marks on the trees from Kenny's eyes, which suggested that those eyes had not dropped calmly back to sleep. Even though the danger was past, Vern and I sat around and were scared for a few minutes, out of politeness to the bear, which had gone out of its way to add a little adventure to our first kid camping trip.

Over the years, Norm, Vern, Kenny, Jake Tift, Willy Piehl, and I, in various combinations that always included me, camped a dozen or more times beneath the rock shelter on Schweitzer Creek. It was there we learned to survive in the woods and to conquer the deadliest beast in the wilderness— the wild-eyed monster that charges not out of the dark woods but out of the night of one's own interior, and goes by the name of Fear. We learned other, simpler lessons, too, such as

Don't Dry Wet Boots over the Fire While You Are Wearing Them!
In demonstrating this lesson to my fellow campers, I propelled
myself some distance into the air and then ricocheted about
the campsite like an erratic rocket, while my feet pressure-
cooked inside my boots. *Don't Dry Wet Boots by the Fire Even
When You Aren't Wearing Them.* Norm, noticing that Vern's boots
had stopped steaming and were now smoking, kicked them
into the cold creek. The sudden change in temperature popped
the toes right off Vern's new boots. The rest of the trip, Vern
walked around grumbling, with his toes protruding from the
front of his boots. He was mad. He said it was uncomfortable,
but I think he was mostly upset because nothing tarnishes a
mountain man's image worse than wearing toeless boots. It
was at the Schweitzer campsite that we learned how to burn
ourselves with hot cookware and hot boots, cut ourselves with
knives and hatchets, gouge ourselves with sharp branches,
bruise ourselves with rocks, and generally damage ourselves
with whatever seemed handy. They were the kinds of lessons
that you need learn only once, and from then on they stick
with you.

By the time we were out of high school, we could disappear
into the mountains for a week or more with packs so light we
scarcely knew they were there. And sometimes they wouldn't
be there, and we would have to backtrack to find them. Vern
and I once spent a week hiking through the Cabinet Mountains, starting out with nothing but our sleeping bags, a pot
and skillet, our knives, an ax, fishing tackle, matches, dried
fruit, dried soup, flour, and a slab of bacon so big that, if the
butcher had left the legs on, it could have walked behind us
on a leash. The first night out, deer sneaked into camp,
dumped over a pack, and ate all the flour and soup right down
to the tiniest speck. The fishing turned out to be not so great
either. By the time the trip was over, we were both sick of
bacon, or as Vern so succinctly put it on the last day, "Oink!"

The mountains have given me everything they promised
back when I heard them whispering to me in my cells at

Farmin School. And much more. I feel more at home in the mountains of Idaho than any other place on earth. A few years ago, when I was hunting with Vern and his wife, Gisela, I fell off the side of a mountain and hurt my leg badly enough that I wasn't sure whether I could hike back to the meeting place. It was in December, with snow on the ground and icy rain falling. So I decided to spend the night at the bottom of the canyon, a place where no one would expect to find me. I made a fire and built a small lean-to furnished with a bed of cedar boughs. I lay there next to the fire for hours, aching, hungry, alone in the dark and the mountains, and I thought, Hey, this is the life!

I should mention here that the incident reported above is referred to throughout northern Idaho as "the night Pat McManus got lost in the woods and was saved by the Boundary County Search and Rescue Team." In some Idaho hunting and fishing circles, the incident is used as a reference point in time:

"You remember when the Plume Creek Fire burned up nine million acres of timber. Well, I was fishing up . . ."

"The Plume Creek Fire? When was that exactly?"

"Ten years before Pat McManus got lost on Twenty Mile Creek."

"Oh, right, I remember now."

The mountains have not always been kind. Several times they have tried to kill me. Once when we were about sixteen, a blizzard caught Vern, Norm, Kenny, and me high in the mountains on the eighteenth of June. Dressed only in lightweight summer clothes and tennis shoes, we thought we'd have to climb into our sleeping bags to keep from freezing to death. The mountain was so steep, though, that we would have had to tie ourselves to trees to keep from sliding back to the bottom of it. Then we came to a ridge and found a trapper's cabin nestled back among the trees. We holed up in the cabin for three days, waiting for the blizzard to blow itself out. That first night as we sat thawing out next to the fire, I distinctly heard the mountain say to itself, "Shucks! I forgot all about that cabin! Well, maybe next time."

Not too long after the trapper's cabin saved our lives, the U.S. Forest Service was infiltrated by an idiot at the management level. The idiot came up with a policy requiring that all the trapper cabins scattered through the national forests be burned. I have many good friends in the Forest Service, and they are bright, dedicated men and women. But the idiot is still roaming around headquarters, probably back in Washington, D.C., trying to give all the good people in the Forest Service a bad name. I wish they'd catch him. Those little cabins provided not only a safe refuge in storms but bits of history. The one we sat out the storm in had this report inscribed on a log: "February 2, 1887. 21 feet of snow on the roof." It wasn't exactly a Samuel Pepys's diary as historical documents go, but it was a fragment of Rocky Mountain history. Yes, I know the snow on the roof was probably only twelve feet deep, but why be picky when you're dealing with posterity?

My closest call in the mountains occurred when I was eighteen. Bob Keough and I were caught by a bad storm twenty miles from the nearest trail. As we inched our way up a precipitous mountain, Bob rolled over on a ledge just above me and lay against his pack staring up into the pounding rain. I climbed up to the ledge and clung precariously to the lip of it. Our heads were a few inches apart. Bob turned to me and matter-of-factly said, "I don't think we're going to make it." The incongruity between his tone and his ominous assessment of our chances for survival struck me as hilarious. Wet, cold, cut, bruised, bleeding, exhausted beyond any limit I had ever even imagined, I laughed so hard I nearly fell off the mountain. Then Bob started laughing. The incongruity multiplied exponentially, as did our laughter. It was insane: two tiny specks adrift in a storm-tossed sea of mountains and beaten to pulps by kindly old homicidal Mother Nature, and the specks laughed. Somehow the laughter recharged us with enough energy to stagger back to what is widely referred to as civilization. Bob was treated by a doctor for a bad cut on his foot and other assorted injuries. I was treated for a ruptured body. But we had beaten the mountains. "Next time," they grumbled, "next time."

Tip: Always include a good supply of humor in your survival kit. Use it liberally for smoothing out rough spots. A dash of it improves the flavor of cold, soggy sandwiches eaten in the rain. It's a big help in climbing mountains, whatever your particular mountain happens to be. It's good for most kinds of pain, although I personally prefer aspirin. I have found humor excellent for defusing panic, calming hysteria, and easing anxiety. Best of all, it's cheap. You can whip up a batch yourself. Simply take a dab of truth, stretch and varnish it, sprinkle with absurdity and a little foolishness, and salt with enough irony to suit your taste. But never point it at anyone you don't intend to hurt. It might go off accidentally. As a youngster, I once directed some humor at a tough kid, and he slugged me into a ditch full of ice water. I must say, though, that it got a good laugh out of him and improved his mood considerably.

FARMING

When I was eleven, Mom remarried. My stepfather, Vic DeMers, was a kind, gentle, and humorous man. Vic had worked in the grocery business most of his life and knew absolutely nothing about farming. That is the only reason I can think of that he decided to turn The Place into a real farm.

Mom had cleared the land herself. She hired men to dynamite the stumps and bulldoze them out of the ground. During summers we would pick up the shattered pieces and pile them in huge stacks and burn them. For lunch we would toss whole potatoes into the coals and let them bake for an hour or so. Then we would drag them out of the coals and eat them with salt. The blackened potatoes looked like rocks, and some-times they were rocks. Potatoes cooked in this fashion were delicious. We were all expert, of course, in scraping off the burnt part.

Once the land was cleared, Mom had the fields planted to wheat and hay, and we were soon growing some of the finest crops in the country. Then Vic moved in. He said all we needed now was some livestock. Pretty soon we were up to our necks in cows, pigs, rabbits, turkeys, and chickens, and up to our ankles in . . . well, I won't go into that. Although we still didn't have much money, we now raised most of our own food: pork, beef, chicken, rabbit, even turkey, and numerous kinds of fruits and vegetables. We caught fish and smoked and canned them. We shot deer, grouse, ducks, pheasants. We cut our own fire-wood. We were almost totally self-sufficient. There was a pe-culiar satisfaction, even smugness, in knowing that no matter what the winter might bring, we would never be cold or hun-gry. All that this wonderful sense of security required was working sixteen hours a day, seven days a week. But I don't wish to give the impression that this was an easy life. Some-times it got hard.

One January, a blizzard froze the temperature at twenty below for three weeks. Drifts piled up so deep between the creek and the barn that the cows couldn't get to water. I was only sixteen, but Vic was now getting on in years—he aged quickly after moving to the farm—so it was decided that I would be the one to haul the water up from the creek for the cows. To do this, I would have to tramp on snowshoes three hundred yards downhill to the creek, fill up a five-gallon can with water, and then carry the water back uphill on a pack-board to the cows.

"Otherwise," Vic said, "the cows will die of thirst before the blizzard blows itself out."

"Yeah," I said, "so let's think about this for a minute, Vic. Just how bad is it, really, if they die of thirst?"

For days I tramped back and forth on snowshoes, hauling

water for a bunch of stupid cows. I would stumble into the barnyard, dump the water in a trough, and a cow would slurp it up in three seconds. "Hit me again, bartender," she would say, "only this time make it a double." Once I dug the toe of a bear-paw snowshoe into a drift and fell forward on my hands and knees. Most of the water in the five-gallon can gurgled down my back before I could right myself. The water instantly coated me with ice from shoulder blades to ankles, and after that, every step I took I crackled. Even school was starting to look better to me than farming. Unfortunately, school had been dismissed because of the blizzard. The principal had decided it would be too hard on the town kids to walk to school in such weather!

Tragically, after I had gone off to college, a similar blizzard killed my stepfather. Vic was found dead in the drifting snow and shrieking wind that we had battled together for nearly a dozen winters. Somehow, I had known that he would never make it alone, and I'm sure he knew it, too. As a Hemingway character remarks, "A man alone doesn't stand a———chance." Hemingway wasn't writing about our little Idaho farm in winter, but he certainly could have been. Nor was he writing about a woman alone. Mom went on living alone at The Place for a dozen more winters. Once, the principal at the school where she taught said, "Mabel, why don't you leave that damn place and move to town."

"I can't," she said. "It's my home."

Idaho winters in those years wore down many a strong man to the point where death didn't seem such a bad alternative. The husband of one of my cousins stumbled in from the cold with an armload of wood one morning and suddenly felt a terminal pain in the vicinity of his heart. "Oh, what the hell," he said with a verbal shrug, and fell over dead. A trapper friend of ours told his wife to watch each night for the light in the window of his cabin high up in the snowy reaches of the Cabinet Mountains. "What should I do if one night I don't see the light?" she asked.

"Go out and get married again," he said.

And there came a night not long afterward when the light didn't go on in the cabin.

After she and Vic were first married, Mom, knowing a good thing when she saw it, quit teaching for a few years. She became a housewife. For the first time, my sister and I discovered that Mom actually knew how to cook. Often, she turned out a fine meal that didn't require us to scrape off any burnt parts. Cooking, however, was never a matter of ultimate concern with her. It was Vic who loved to cook. A Frenchman, his specialty was French cuisine, dishes with impossible-to-pronounce French names. Mom, the Troll, and I had to invent our own names for them. His fish stew became "Buoy Bess." Another stew became "Paddle Your Own Canoe." I didn't care much for either of them. "Cripes," I'd say, "not Paddle Your Own Canoe for supper again!" What I liked most were Vic's crepes suzette, cooked on top of the stove, and his gros crepes, baked in the oven. The suzettes were the typical crepes of today, and were filled with jam or cheese or anything else handy. The gros crepes were huge, airy, golden pancakes containing strips of crisp bacon. We coated them with melted butter, maple sugar, and sometimes whipped cream and crushed walnuts. We had come a long way from milk toast and gruel.

There was no such thing as cholesterol in those days, which was fortunate. Otherwise, our diet would have been lethal. A typical day's meals would go something like this: For breakfast we would have bacon and eggs and toast smeared with home-made butter. For lunch we'd have fried ham and a vegetable drenched with butter and glasses of whole milk that was half cream. For supper we'd have steak, butter-drenched vegetables, and shortcake covered with great globs of whipped cream. Just thinking about that diet now can clog my arteries.

One aspect of farming I had trouble getting used to was killing. A terrible amount of killing goes on at a subsistence farm. Even before Vic arrived on the scene, we executed our own chickens. Gram operated the guillotine, a double-bitted ax, but I had to run down the victims and haul them over to the chopping block. The chicken would be yelling, "Keep away from that old lady with the ax—she's crazy!" My dog, Strange, would dance about barking and yelping happily, for there were few things he enjoyed more than a good execution. Gram would shout out orders. "Fetch me that chicken and

 don't be all day about it. Land sakes, if you ain't the slowest child! Now hold him down on the choppin' block, while I whack his head off." I would close my eyes as Gram raised the wavering ax over her head. *Chunk!* I'd open my eyes. The ax would be sunk into the chopping block a few inches from my hands. "Drat!" Gram would mutter. "Durn chicken moved. Hold him

steady now, you hear me, boy! I'm gonna take another whack at him. Keep your eyes open, dang it, so you can see what you're doin'." I'd close my eyes. Holding a chicken for Gram to chop its head off was a lot like getting a cigarette shot out of your mouth by a trick-shot artist with a bad aim.

After Vic arrived, the farm turned into a major killing ground—chickens, rabbits, turkeys, hogs, and steers bit the dust one after another and sometimes in twos and threes. All of them I had helped raise from infancy. I named them, talked to them, played with them. Then early one morning Vic and I would show up at a creature's pen. "Hi, guys," it would say, "What's up?" What was up was its number. For me, killing some of the animals was like killing a close friend or at least a moderately distant relative, say maybe a second cousin who had come to visit for the summer. "Well, we're running a little low on meat. Best we hit Cousin Joe Bob in the head." One summer I tried raising some turkeys, but one by one they got picked off by coyotes or their own stupidity, until I was down to one. I named him Beaky and taught him tricks, such as running to me every time I called him by name and held out a can of grain. Beaky grew big and fat and beautiful, and then came Thanksgiving. We all sat down to a delicious feast. I was delighted by the sight of all the fabulous dishes on the table, the mashed potatoes and gravy, the salads, cranberries, pickled crab apples, olives, stuffed celery, sauces and jellies, even the vegetables, and particularly the huge, golden turkey. The rest of the family, however, seemed unusually quiet and somewhat nervous. We ate and ate and ate, in typical Thanksgiving style, and soon everyone was laughing, talking, and carrying on as if everything were normal. Finally, I pushed back from the table and said, "Wow! I'm stuffed! I couldn't eat another bite."

"You sure?" Mom said. "How about another helping of Beak . . . uh . . . turkey?"

"What?" I said, staring at the carved-up turkey carcass in horror. "What did you say?"

"T-turkey," Mom said, glancing guiltily at Vic. "I said 'turkey.'"

"Uh, it's like this, Pat," Vic mumbled. "You see, Beaky was getting along in months, and so we thought, rather than let him suffer the ravages of old age, that . . ."

"*YOU . . . MEAN . . . WE . . . JUST . . . ATE . . . BEAKY?*"

I knew my folks were a hard lot but I hadn't realized they were . . . *cannibals*!

STRANGE

*T*his memoir would be incomplete without further mention of my dog, Strange. I have written about him often in other places, and readers ask if he was a real dog. It's a question I'm never quite sure how to answer. In many respects, Strange certainly resembled a real dog. He had a doglike tail, for example, and floppy ears, and was pretty much covered all over with dog hair, except when he tangled with the timber wolves our neighbors employed mainly for chasing kids on their bicycles. After these encounters, he was only partially covered with dog hair.

Strange was essentially a bully and, like most bullies, also a coward. His assaults by the wolves were usually a result of some miscalculation on his part. He would stand at our property-line fence and shout obscenities at the wolves, supposing that the wolves were familiar with trespass laws and would not pursue him beyond the fence and onto his own land. Seeing that he had misjudged the wolves' legal acumen, he would turn and race for the safety of the house, his stubby legs churning frantically as the tall wolves drifted along, playfully nipping at his rear and assorted other parts of his anatomy. Unable to break his habit of teasing the wolves, Strange apparently resigned himself to the general appearance of something that buzzards had sampled but hadn't seriously considered eating. I suspect Strange was of the opinion, after these encounters, that he had taught the wolves a good lesson, and that it would be some time before they risked messing with him again. He was a small but arrogant dog.

When Strange first showed up at our place as a young dog, my mother named him Stranger, probably in the hope that he was just passing through. He stayed on for a dozen years, and his name was eventually shortened to Strange, which, given his character, seemed much more appropriate. He loved trouble of all kinds and sought it out at every opportunity. If he couldn't find trouble, he invented some. He had a gastric turbulence of the highest odor. Once my mother invited some of her teacher friends out to play pinochle. Strange, inflated like a balloon, sneaked into the house and sauntered beneath the card table. "Oops," he said, deflating, "sorry, ladies." The stricken guests, stripped of even the pretense of etiquette, rose gagging, choking, and fanning the air with their hands, after which they staggered blindly about, looking for an open door or window. To make matters worse, the dog, no doubt snickering, slipped away undetected, leaving the guests to wonder about the identity of the offending culprit. Strange was a major social liability, and my mother did not much care for him, sometimes even suggesting that he be done away with. As she put it after her disrupted card party, "I'll killlll that dog with my bare hands!"

I tried to defend Strange. "He's just not an inside dog."

"He ain't even an outside dog!" Gram growled.

I once asked Gram how long dogs lived. "Too long," she said, staring at Strange, "too long."

Gram and Strange didn't get on at all. He complained constantly about her cooking. She would collect the table scraps after dinner, including such things as boiled greens and mashed turnips, and dump it all in his dish. Strange would sniff at the blob, look up at Gram, and say, "You expect me to eat this slop?" She was naturally offended that a dog would refuse to eat her cooking. I suggested to Gram that Strange would like her cooking better if she sorted out the foods he didn't like from those he did. Fortunately, I was a quick and agile child and managed to escape with my life.

As I have mentioned in other writings, Strange had only two jobs, to protect the chickens and assault burglars, but he could never keep the two tasks straight in his head. He was constantly attacking chickens, claiming they had provoked him in some way. He wasn't much of a fighter, though, and the average hen could lick him two out of three times. Conversely, he would greet dangerous-looking tramps at the gate and invite them in for a meal. "The old lady's cooking don't taste like much, pal," he'd explain, "but it's filling."

Early in his residence with us, Strange went berserk and killed a skunk. The fight was long and noisy and savage, and raged all over our backyard. When the battle was over, Strange picked up the dead skunk and put it on display atop our well cover. It was a Sunday and we were just getting dressed to go to church. But the very air was stiff with the stench of the skunk, which had fired its whole arsenal at Strange. The smell seemed to permeate every fiber of our being. It was so strong as to border on physical pain. I was furious with Strange, knowing that he had brought on this suffering for no reason other than he had some small grudge against the skunk. "This is terrible!" Mom moaned. "We smell like skunk ourselves. There's no way we can go to church now!"

"Good boy," I said to Strange. Dogs will be dogs.

Eventually, Strange grew old and lame and crotchety, and Mom decided we should get another dog. Somewhere she acquired a white pup named Tippy, because he had a brown tip on his tail. As he grew older, the tip disappeared, leading many people to ask, "How come you call him Tippy?" By then, most of the family had forgotten why we called him Tippy in the first place and could only reply with a shrug, yet another reason for folks to think our family somewhat eccentric. Although we never had him officially tested, Tippy probably ranked number one in the nation for canine stupidity. This turned out to have its advantages, because Strange immediately started trying to teach Tippy the ropes.

"Okay, Tip, listen to me now," Strange would instruct. "Say you whack a skunk. What's your average dog gonna do when he snuffs a skunk? He's gonna leave it right where it lays, okay, but that ain't the way we do it around here. No, what we do is carry the stiff over and drop it on top of the well. You got that?"

"Hunh?" Tippy would say, scratching his ear with a hind foot.

It was Tippy who inadvertently brought about Strange's demise. One of the neighbor's wolves was trotting across our field, minding his own business, when Tippy took it into his head to read the trespasser the riot act. The wolf snarled once, and Tippy flipped over on his back, quivering and shaking, a craven smile of subservience on his face. Perhaps it was this pitiful spectacle that disgusted Strange to the point of rage, although not many things disgusted him. Whatever the reason, he hit the wolf at full speed right in the throat, and they disappeared into a cloud of dust and spinning dog parts. When the dust cleared, the wolf staggered off toward home, but

Strange remained on the ground. I carried him back to the house. "I don't know what came over me," he said. "I must have gone bonkers." He lingered for a few hours wrapped up in a blanket on the floor. After a bit he crawled over to a window and looked out. "A dog like me should live for a thousand years," he said. Then he died.

Tippy waited alone by the supper dish that night while Gram slopped in the leftovers. "Hey, terrific grub, Granny!" he yelped.

"Good dog!" Gram said.

IN CLOSING

Well, that's about it for this memoir. I have deliberately avoided mentioning some of my close associates of early years—the old woodsman Rancid Crabtree, Crazy Eddie Muldoon, Retch Sweeney, Henry P. Grogan, and many others. I am often asked if the fictional characters Rancid, Crazy Eddie, Retch, and the others are based in part on real people. They are, and the real people are well known to my lifetime associates. But there's a problem in dealing with my real people in a work of nonfiction, which this memoir pretty much is. First of all, I would have to sterilize the real people so much for public consumption that their skins would fall off, and they would dissolve once again into fiction. So I thought it best if I left them alone. Mothers should thank me for doing so.

BREADS

Baking Powder Biscuits

2 cups flour
1 tablespoon sugar
4 teaspoons baking powder
1 teaspoon salt
½ cup vegetable shortening
1 beaten egg
⅔ cup milk

Sift dry ingredients. Cut in shortening until mixture resembles cornmeal. Combine egg and milk; add to flour mixture all at once. Stir with fork until mixture holds together. Place on floured surface and knead lightly 8 to 10 times. Roll out to approximately ¾-inch thickness and cut with 2-inch cutter. Place biscuits on ungreased sheet and bake at 425° for 12 minutes, or until golden in color. *Makes 15 biscuits.*

Griddle Scones

Mom occasionally made us griddle scones for Sunday breakfast, but we never recognized them. We thought they were mutated muffins. Good, though.

2 cups sifted flour
1 tablespoon baking powder
1 tablespoon sugar
$\frac{1}{2}$ teaspoon salt
$\frac{1}{4}$ cup butter or margarine
2 eggs
$\frac{1}{3}$ cup milk

Sift flour again with baking powder, sugar, and salt. Cut in butter or margarine. Beat eggs and milk together and stir into the dry ingredients, blending thoroughly with as few strokes as possible. Turn out onto lightly floured board and knead about 5 times. Roll out to $\frac{1}{2}$-inch thickness and cut into 2-inch rounds. Preheat griddle to 325°. Place scones on ungreased surface. Cook about 10 minutes, turn, and cook 10 minutes on other side. Serve hot. *Makes 14 to 18 scones.*

Sour Cream Coffee Cake

$\frac{3}{4}$ cup pecans, finely chopped
$1\frac{1}{2}$ teaspoons cinnamon
$\frac{1}{2}$ teaspoon nutmeg

¾ cup sugar
1¼ cups sugar
¾ cup butter or margarine
3 eggs
1½ cups sour cream
3 cups flour
1½ teaspoons baking powder
1½ teaspoons baking soda
1½ teaspoons vanilla

In small bowl, combine pecans, cinnamon, nutmeg, and ¾ cup sugar. In a large bowl, beat 1¼ cups sugar and butter or margarine at medium speed with electric beater until combined. Add eggs and beat. Add sour cream, flour, baking powder, baking soda, and vanilla. Blend at low speed, then 3 minutes on medium speed. Heat oven to 350°. Grease 10-inch tube pan. Spread ⅓ dough in pan; sprinkle with ⅓ nut mixture. Continue with second and third layers of dough and nut mixture, ending with nut mixture on top. Bake for 60 to 65 minutes. Cool in pan on wire rack. *Serves 12.*

Mrs. Whipple's Dumplings

2 cups flour
2 teaspoons salt
5 teaspoons baking powder
1 egg
2 tablespoons salad oil
Cold water to moisten ingredients

Sift flour, salt, and baking powder together. Beat egg and oil together with ¼ cup cold water and add to flour mixture. Continue to add cold water, a tablespoon at a time, until all ingredients are moistened. Drop into hot stock (soup, stew, etc.) with tablespoon. Cover and cook on low heat for 20 minutes. *Makes 6 large dumplings.*

Apple Muffins

2 eggs
1 cup salad oil
1 cup sugar
1 teaspoon vanilla
2 cups flour
2 teaspoons cinnamon
1/2 teaspoon nutmeg
Dash of cloves
1/4 teaspoon salt
1 teaspoon baking soda
4 cups peeled and chopped apples
3/4 cup chopped walnuts or pecans

Beat eggs until foamy; add oil, sugar, and vanilla. Mix dry ingredients together and stir into egg mixture until well blended. Stir in apples and nuts. Pour into greased muffin tins and bake at 350° for 15 to 20 minutes, or until done. *Makes 16 muffins.*

Cornmeal Muffins

2 eggs
2/3 cup milk
1/3 cup melted butter or margarine

1¼ cups flour
¼ cup sugar
3 teaspoons baking powder
1 teaspoon salt
¾ cup yellow cornmeal

Beat eggs, milk, and butter or margarine until well blended. Stir in flour, sugar, baking powder, and salt; add cornmeal. Stir just until blended and dry ingredients are moist. Spoon into greased muffin tins and bake at 425° for 20 to 25 minutes, or until done. *Makes 12 muffins.*

Huckleberry Muffins

½ cup butter or margarine
1 cup sugar
2 eggs
1¾ cups sifted flour
1 teaspoon baking powder
¾ teaspoon baking soda
¼ teaspoon salt
¼ teaspoon nutmeg
¼ teaspoon cloves
¾ cup buttermilk
1 cup huckleberries, fresh or frozen

Cream butter or margarine, sugar, and eggs together. Stir in dry ingredients alternating with buttermilk. Fold in well-drained huckleberries. Pour into greased muffin tins and bake at 375° for 20 to 25 minutes, or until done. Dip in topping (see p. 66). *Makes 12 to 15 muffins.*

TOPPING:

1/2 cup melted butter or margarine
3/4 cup sugar
2 tablespoons grated orange rind

Mix sugar and grated orange rind together. While muffins are still warm, dip tops in melted butter or margarine, then into sugar–orange rind mixture.

Mom's Cornmeal Mush

1 1/4 cups cornmeal
1 teaspoon salt
2 1/2 cups boiling water

Sprinkle cornmeal gradually into boiling salted water; stir constantly until mixture boils. Allow to boil for 4 or 5 minutes, being careful not to get burned when it bubbles up. Cook on very low heat until mixture is thick. *Serves 4.*

*W*e got a lot of mileage out of cornmeal mush. In the evenings it often served as dessert with sugar and cream on top. For breakfast and lunch, it was served the same way. If we were lucky and some was left over, it was poured into a greased loaf pan and let set overnight in a cool place. The next morning we had:

Mom's Fried Cornmeal Mush

Cut cornmeal mush into ½-inch-thick slices. Dip each side in flour and fry in bacon fat until golden brown. Serve with butter and syrup. *Serves 4.*

*M*y aunt Verda made the world's best noodles. She was a plump and permanently cheerful lady, at whose house I spent a good portion of my childhood. There was always a great abundance of wonderful food there. Aunt Verda's mission in life apparently was to feed people, and she worked at it twelve hours a day. She belonged to the high-calorie school of cooking. You could gain five pounds just walking by her house. She transformed even the most humble foods into gourmet treats, merely by having touched them. She once gave me a slice of homemade bread so delicious I remember it after forty years. I usually don't find a slice of bread all that memorable either.

Aunt Verda's Noodles

   9 egg yolks
   ½ eggshell of water
   1 tablespoon salt
   Enough flour to make a stiff dough

Beat the egg yolks slightly with a fork and add water. Add salt and stir in flour with a spoon until you have a very, very stiff dough. Remove from bowl and knead 5 times. Roll out on a heavily floured board as thin as possible, keeping the dough well floured as you roll it out. The thinner the dough, the better the noodles. Roll as you would for cinnamon rolls and, using a very sharp knife, slice through the rolls, making noodles as thin as desired. Toss noodles as you cut them, and let them set to dry, tossing several times as they dry. Cook in boiling, salted broth. Noodles can be used immediately or placed in bags and frozen. *Serves 8.*

Buttermilk Pancakes

3 eggs
1²/₃ cups buttermilk
1¹/₂ cups sifted flour
1 tablespoon sugar
1 teaspoon baking powder
1 teaspoon baking soda
¹/₂ teaspoon salt
3 tablespoons melted butter or margarine

Separate eggs and beat whites until stiff. Beat egg yolks with fork. Mix all ingredients together except egg whites, then fold in beaten egg whites. Bake on medium-hot, greased griddle. *Makes enough pancakes for 4 hungry people.*

Gram's Huckleberry Pancakes

1¹/₃ cups flour
¹/₂ teaspoon baking soda

1 teaspoon salt
1 tablespoon sugar
1 egg
1 tablespoon salad oil
1 cup milk
4 tablespoons melted butter or margarine
1 cup sour cream
1 cup huckleberries, fresh or frozen

Combine dry ingredients; add egg, oil, milk, and butter or margarine. Blend sour cream into mixture until batter is smooth. Pour batter on hot, greased griddle. Scatter huckleberries on top. *Makes 9 medium-sized pancakes.*

Mom's Maple Syrup

Mom made syrup for our pancakes. Store-bought was too expensive.

1 cup white sugar
3 cups packed brown sugar
2 cups water
²/₃ cup light corn syrup
2 teaspoons mapleine

Bring sugars, water, and syrup almost to a boil. Remove from heat and add mapleine. *Makes 5 cups.*

Pat's Perky Popovers

1 cup flour
½ teaspoon salt

3 eggs
1 cup milk
3 tablespoons salad oil

Mix flour and salt. Beat eggs, milk, and salad oil with a beater until just blended. Pour mixture over flour and salt. Beat with spoon until smooth. Do not overbeat. Pour batter into greased custard cups until half full. Bake at 400° for 50 minutes. Five minutes before they have finished baking, poke small hole in top of each popover to let steam escape. Serve hot. *Makes 8 large popovers.*

Sassy Applesauce Bread

³/₄ cup sugar
1 cup thick applesauce
¹/₃ cup salad oil
2 eggs
3 tablespoons milk
2 cups sifted flour
1 teaspoon baking soda
¹/₂ teaspoon baking powder
¹/₄ teaspoon salt
¹/₂ teaspoon cinnamon
¹/₄ teaspoon nutmeg
³/₄ cup seedless raisins or
  chopped walnuts

Combine sugar, applesauce, salad oil, eggs, and milk. Sift dry ingredients, except raisins or walnuts, and add to first mixture. Beat until blended. Stir in raisins or nuts. Pour batter into greased and floured pan (9 × 5 inches) and bake at 350° for 50 minutes or until bread is done. *Makes 1 loaf.*

Banana Bread

¾ cup sugar
½ cup melted butter or margarine
2 eggs, beaten
3 bananas, mashed
2 cups flour
1 teaspoon baking soda
¼ cup chopped walnuts

Cream sugar and melted butter or margarine. Add eggs and mashed bananas. Stir in flour, baking soda, and nuts. Pour into greased and floured pan (9 × 5 inches). Bake at 350° for 30 to 40 minutes. Serve with cream cheese, if desired. *Makes 1 loaf.*

Beer Bread

3 cups self-rising flour
3 tablespoons sugar
1 can (12 ounces) beer

Mix flour and sugar. Add beer and stir well. Pour batter into a greased pan (9 × 5 inches). Cover and let rise for 1 hour at room temperature. Bake at 350° for 1 hour or until lightly browned. *Makes 1 loaf.*

Corn Bread

1 egg
2/3 cup milk
1/3 cup salad oil
1 1/4 cups flour
3/4 cup cornmeal
2 tablespoons sugar
4 1/2 teaspoons baking powder
1 teaspoon salt

Beat egg with a fork. Add milk and salad oil and stir together. Mix dry ingredients, add egg mixture, and blend until flour is moistened. Pour into greased pan (8 × 8 inches) and bake at 425° for 25 to 30 minutes. *Serves 6.*

Mom's Crackling Corn Bread

1 cup cornmeal
1 cup flour
1 teaspoon baking soda
1 teaspoon salt
1 cup buttermilk
2 eggs, beaten
1/3 cup salad oil
1/2 cup crisp cracklings (see Mom's
    Cracklings, page 239)

Mix cornmeal, flour, baking soda, and salt. Add buttermilk, eggs, oil, and cracklings. Stir just until combined. Pour into greased pan (9 x 9 inches) and bake at 425° for 20 minutes. *Serves 6.*

Hobo Bread

2 cups seedless raisins or dried fruit
2 cups boiling water
4 teaspoons baking soda
4 cups flour
1¼ cups white sugar
½ cup packed brown sugar
4 tablespoons vegetable shortening
1 teaspoon salt

The evening before, mix raisins or dried fruit of choice, boiling water, and baking soda, and let them set overnight. The next morning, add remaining ingredients. Blend well. Pour into 2 greased and floured 1-pound coffee cans. Bake at 350° for 1½ hours. *Makes 2 loaves.*

Irish Soda Bread

5 cups all-purpose flour
1½ teaspoons baking powder
¼ teaspoon baking soda
¼ teaspoon salt
1 tablespoon caraway seeds
¼ cup salad oil
2 cups buttermilk
9 ounces seedless raisins
1 egg
1 teaspoon sugar
1 tablespoon water

Stir first eight ingredients together, being sure not to overmix. Divide dough into 3 round loaves. Cut an X in the top of each loaf and place on greased cookie sheet. Brush with an egg wash made by beating together egg, sugar, and water. Let set 15 minutes. Bake at 375° for 30 to 35 minutes. *Makes 3 loaves.*

Zucchini Bread

3 eggs
1¾ cups sugar
1 cup salad oil
2 teaspoons vanilla
2 tablespoons grated orange peel
2 cups unpeeled, grated, raw
   zucchini squash
3 cups flour
1 teaspoon salt
1 teaspoon baking soda
¼ teaspoon baking powder
2 teaspoons cinnamon
½ cup seedless raisins or nuts

Beat eggs until light. Add sugar and beat well. Stir in oil, vanilla, orange peel, and zucchini squash. Sift and add dry ingredients, stirring in well. Add raisins or nuts. Turn into two greased and floured pans (9 x 5 inches) and bake at 350° for 50 to 60 minutes or until bread tests done. *Makes 2 loaves.*

High-on-the-Hog Scrapple

When the pig was butchered in the fall, we had scrapple frequently after the sausage was made.

Make cornmeal mush using 3 cups water, 1 teaspoon salt, and 1½ cups cornmeal. Sauté ½ pound sausage with a little onion until thoroughly cooked. Drain and add to the cornmeal mush. Pour into greased loaf pan and let set overnight in a cool place until firm. Cut ¾-inch slices, dip in flour, and sauté in bacon fat or lard until golden brown. Serve with butter or margarine and syrup. *Makes 12 slices.*

Bran Bread

2 packages dry yeast
½ cup warm water
2 cups All-bran cereal
4 cups hot water
½ cup sugar
3 tablespoons molasses
2 tablespoons vegetable shortening
2 tablespoons salt
6 to 7 cups white flour

Dissolve yeast in ½ cup warm water. Stir All-bran cereal into 4 cups hot water and let set 5 minutes. Combine All-bran, sugar, molasses, shortening, and salt. Stir yeast mixture into bran mixture. Add white flour until dough is stiff enough to knead. Knead until smooth, about 8 to 10 minutes. Place in greased bowl and let rise for an hour. Punch down. Shape into

2 loaves and place in greased pans (9 x 5 inches). Bake at 375° for 25 minutes or until loaves sound hollow when thumped. *Makes 2 loaves.*

Honey Whole-Wheat Bread

¾ cup honey
3 cups hot water
2 packages dry yeast
1 tablespoon salt
¼ cup salad oil
About 6 cups whole wheat flour

Add honey to hot water, stir together, and let cool to luke-warm. Add yeast and stir. Leave 5 to 10 minutes to froth. Stir in salt and oil; gradually add the flour. Mix all together until the mixture forms a ball, adding extra flour if necessary. Knead for 5 to 10 minutes until the dough is smooth. Cover and let rise until doubled in size. Punch down the dough, shape into 2 large loaves, and place in greased pans (9 x 5 inches). The extra dough can be made into rolls and placed in greased pan (8 x 8 inches). Cover pans and let rise until doubled in size. The dough is ready to bake if it retains an indent when pressed with a floured finger. Bake at 375° for 35 to 45 minutes or until loaves sound hollow when thumped. *Makes 2 loaves and 10 rolls.*

Rye Bread

4 cups scalded milk, cooled to lukewarm
2 cakes yeast or 2 packages dry yeast

½ cup sugar
4 tablespoons caraway seeds
5 cups water
4 cups rye flour
1 cup molasses
5 teaspoons salt
¼ cup vegetable shortening
White flour as needed

This recipe calls for two separate mixtures to be made and then combined later. For the first mixture, make a spongy mass with milk, yeast, and sugar, and set aside. To make the second mixture, boil caraway seeds in water and pour over the rye flour, molasses, salt, and shortening. Stir until combined thoroughly and let stand covered until cool enough to add to first mixture.

After combining the two mixtures, add white flour until dough is of consistency to knead. Knead until smooth. Place in greased bowl and turn once to grease top. Cover and let rise until doubled in bulk. Punch down and shape into 4 loaves. Place in greased pans (9 x 5 inches) and let rise again until doubled. This dough is always stickier than white bread dough. Bake at 400° for 10 minutes and 325° for 20 minutes. *Makes 4 loaves.*

Chunk of Cheese Bread

1¾ cups water
2 teaspoons salt

½ cup cornmeal
½ cup molasses
3 tablespoons butter or margarine
1 package dry yeast
½ cup warm water
About 5 cups white flour
⅘ pound Cheddar cheese
Cornmeal

Combine 1¾ cups water, salt, and ½ cup cornmeal in saucepan. Bring to boil, stirring constantly, and cook until slightly thickened. Remove from heat; add molasses and butter or margarine. Stir and let cool to lukewarm. Dissolve yeast in ½ cup warm water. Add the cornmeal mixture to yeast and stir well. Gradually add about 5 cups flour and knead to a smooth, elastic dough. Let rise until doubled in bulk. Cut cheese into ½-inch cubes. Place dough on a surface which has been sprinkled with cornmeal. Work the cheese into the dough a little at a time. Divide dough into 2 equal parts. Shape each piece into a round loaf, covering all the cheese. Place loaves in two greased 9-inch pie pans. Cover and let rise until doubled. Bake at 350° for 40 to 45 minutes. *Makes 2 loaves.*

White Yeast Bread

1 teaspoon sugar
1 cup lukewarm water
2 packages dry yeast
2 cups milk, scalded
3 teaspoons salt
⅓ cup sugar
9 cups white flour, approximately
¼ cup melted butter or margarine

Add 1 teaspoon sugar to lukewarm water. Stir in yeast and let set until yeast begins working. Put scalded milk, salt, and ⅓ cup sugar in large bowl; cool to lukewarm. Add yeast mixture, and gradually stir in 4 cups flour. Beat until smooth. Beat in cooled, melted butter or margarine. Add enough flour to make a smooth, soft dough. Let dough rest 10 minutes, covered. Knead dough until smooth and elastic, adding more flour as needed. Place dough in greased bowl and cover. Let rise in warm place until doubled. When dough has risen enough, the dent made by pressing a finger into dough remains. Punch dough down, and divide into 3 equal pieces. Shape into loaves and place in 3 greased pans (9 x 5 inches). Cover and let rise until doubled. Bake at 425° for 30 minutes, or until bread is golden brown and sounds hollow when thumped. Remove from pans and brush with melted butter or margarine. *Makes 3 loaves.*

Indian Fried Bread

When white bread dough is ready for shaping into loaves (see p. 78), pinch off small pieces and flatten in your hand. Heat 3 inches salad oil to 375° and drop in pieces of dough. Fry until puffed and golden, turning once. We preferred this bread to any other, especially spread with butter and huckleberry jam.

Dinner Rolls

2 cups milk
2 packages dry yeast
2 tablespoons sugar
7½ cups flour
½ cup butter or margarine

⅔ cup sugar
2 eggs, beaten
1 teaspoon salt

Scald milk and let cool. Dissolve yeast and 2 tablespoons sugar in lukewarm milk. Add 3¼ cups flour to yeast mixture to make a sponge. Let rise until light. Cream butter or margarine and ⅔ cup sugar; add to yeast mixture. Add eggs, salt, and enough flour to make a soft dough, approximately 4¼ cups. Knead until smooth. Let rise until doubled in bulk. Punch down and shape into 50 rolls. Place in 2 greased pans (11 x 13 inches). Let rise until doubled. Bake at 375° for 15 minutes, or until brown. *Makes 50 rolls.*

Rich and Highly Fattening Dinner Rolls

2 packages dry yeast
1 tablespoon sugar
½ cup lukewarm water
1 cup milk
½ cup melted butter or margarine
½ cup sugar
1 teaspoon salt
4 eggs, lightly beaten
About 5 cups flour

Dissolve yeast and 1 tablespoon sugar in lukewarm water. Set aside. Scald milk, add butter or margarine, and let cool. Add ½ cup sugar, salt, and beaten eggs. Stir yeast into milk mixture. Stir in 4½ cups flour and continue to add flour until you have a soft dough. Knead until smooth. Place in greased bowl and turn once to grease top. Cover and let rise until doubled in bulk. Punch down and make into 36 rolls. Place in 2 greased pans (8 x 10 inches) and let rise until doubled. Bake at 400° for 15 minutes, or until golden brown. *Makes 36 rolls.*

Refrigerator Rolls

2 packages dry yeast
2 cups warm water
½ cup sugar
¼ cup soft vegetable shortening
2 eggs
2 teaspoons salt
⅔ cup nonfat dry milk (not mixed)
6 to 7 cups flour

Dissolve yeast in warm water. Add sugar and let set until yeast starts working. Stir in shortening, eggs, and salt. Mix in dry milk and flour until dough is soft and pliable. Knead until dough is elastic, about 5 minutes. Put in greased, covered bowl and store in refrigerator 4 or 5 hours or overnight. Use within one day. Take out of refrigerator and shape into desired type of rolls. Let rise until doubled in bulk. Bake at 375° for 15 to 20 minutes, or until golden brown. *Makes about 24 large rolls.*

Raised Scones

2 cups milk
1 package dry yeast

3 tablespoons sugar
1/4 cup melted vegetable shortening
3 1/2 to 4 1/2 cups flour
2 teaspoons salt
Salad oil for frying

Scald milk and cool to lukewarm. Dissolve yeast in milk and add sugar. Let stand until foamy. Stir in shortening. Add flour and salt; mix until smooth. Let rise about 2 hours. Punch down and roll on a floured board to about 1/4-inch thickness. Cut in rounds and fry in 4 inches of oil heated to 375° until brown, turning once. Serve hot with honey and butter or margarine. *Makes 14 to 16 scones.*

*E*lvera Klein of Boise, Idaho, has elevated sourdough cooking to a major art form. Many of the following recipes have been pilfered from Elvera's *Creative Sourdough Recipes*, which can be ordered directly from her. See Acknowledgments for address.

HINTS FOR COOKING WITH SOURDOUGH

*I*t's best to make up starter the night before using it; this way it will have several hours to work. If the starter you are using has been refrigerated, be sure to let it come to room temperature first. (If you seldom use your starter, it can be refrigerated.)

Make up the amount of starter you will need, but be sure to return 1 cup starter to your container, cover container and bowl with clean cloth, and let work. This way you will be sure not to forget about saving some starter.

Keep your sourdough in an oversized container with a loose cover such as foil. It needs room to grow and air to breathe. The sourdough will work as long as it is kept in a moderately warm area, and the longer it works, the better it will be.

If your sourdough hasn't been used for a couple of weeks, discard half of it and add ½ cup warm water and ¾ cup flour. Be sure to mix well and leave in a warm place to work.

Don't use a metal container or spoon for your sourdough. A ceramic or glass container and wooden spoon work best.

When your batter is too stiff to be workable, add a small amount of warm water, keeping in mind that as the mixture works, it will become thinner. Always use water in making sourdough, never milk; and never return to your container any sourdough to which other ingredients have been added.

Baking soda is used as a sweetener in sourdough, and sugar is used for browning. When making pancakes or waffles, be sure to add baking soda dissolved in water last, and be ready to cook them immediately. The baking soda causes a foaming action and makes whatever you are working with light.

It takes longer for sourdough products to bake, so they should be tested before taking them from the oven.

Gram left her sourdough pot on top of the warming oven on the old wood range, and our kitchen was always filled with a yeasty aroma that reminded us of fresh bread coming from the oven. The longer sourdough works, the more delicious and sour it becomes. Some people are still using starter they had fifty years ago.

There are many ways to make a starter. The easiest is to borrow some from a friend; it only takes a small amount. Mix 2 cups flour, 2 tablespoons sugar, and 2 cups water. Add to the starter, and let it set in a warm place for two or three days, or until sour.

Potato Sourdough Starter

If no starter is available, it is easy to make from scratch.

    2 medium potatoes
    1–2 cups water
    2 cups flour
    2 tablespoons sugar
    Pinch of dry yeast

Boil 2 medium potatoes until they fall apart; mash and cool. Add enough water to make 2 cups potato water. Mix with flour, sugar, and yeast. Cover with clean cloth and let set in warm spot to work—3 or 4 days or until it has a definite sour smell and is bubbly. Stir several times a day.

Elvera Klein's Sourdough Starter

    1 package dry yeast
    2¹/₂ cups warm water
    2 cups flour
    1 tablespoon sugar

Dissolve yeast in warm water. Stir in flour and sugar. Beat well. Cover with cheesecloth and let stand in a warm place for 2 or 3 days. Stir down 2 or 3 times a day, as this helps to activate starter. When ready to use, the starter should be bubbly and have a delicate sour aroma. An active, bubbly starter is essential for a quality sourdough product.

Sourdough French Bread

2 cups sourdough starter (see p. 84)
1 tablespoon sugar
1 tablespoon salad oil
Pinch of salt
5½ to 6 cups white flour

Combine starter, sugar, oil, salt, and 5 cups flour. Mix well. Pour out on floured board and knead, adding flour as needed, until you have a smooth, elastic dough. Allow dough to rest for 10 minutes. Shape into 2 long, narrow rolls and place on greased cookie sheet. Make slashes in bread about 2 inches apart with sharp knife. Let rise until a little over doubled in bulk. Bake at 475° for 10 minutes. Reduce heat to 375° and bake for 30 minutes. Halfway through baking, brush with cold water. *Makes 2 loaves.*

Sourdough White Bread

5 to 6 cups white flour
⅓ cup instant dry milk
3 teaspoons sugar
1 teaspoon salt
1 package dry yeast
1 cup water
2 tablespoons butter or margarine
1½ cups sourdough starter (see p. 84)

Combine 2 cups flour, instant dry milk, sugar, salt, and yeast. Heat water and butter or margarine until very warm. Add warm water and sourdough starter to flour mixture; blend until moistened. Beat with a mixer for 3 minutes at medium speed. Continue to add flour, $1/2$ cup at a time, until dough can be kneaded. Turn out on floured board and knead for 10 minutes or until smooth and elastic, adding more flour if needed. Place dough in greased bowl, turn over to grease top, cover, and let rise in warm place until light and doubled in size. Punch dough down and allow to rest covered for 10 minutes. Divide dough in 2 pieces and shape into round loaves. Slash an X on top of each loaf. Place on a greased cookie sheet, cover, and let rise in warm place until doubled. Bake at 400° for 20 to 30 minutes or until loaves are brown and sound hollow when thumped. *Makes 2 loaves.*

Sourdough Pancakes

1 cup sourdough starter
  (see p. 84)
2 cups flour
1 egg
1 teaspoon sugar
$1/2$ teaspoon baking soda
1 tablespoon water

Mix sourdough starter and flour with enough warm water to make a thick batter. Let work overnight.

The next morning, take out 1 cup of the mixture and save. To remaining sourdough, add egg and sugar. Mix well. Stir baking soda into water and fold into batter just before baking. If the batter is too thick, add a little more water. Drop batter on moderately hot, greased griddle. *Serves 3.*

Elvera's Swedish Sourdough Coffee Ring

1 cup sourdough starter (see p. 84)
³/₄ cup warm water
1 cup flour

Place sourdough starter in a large bowl. Add water alternately with flour and beat well. Return 1 cup starter to the sourdough pot. Cover both and set in a warm place for 2 or 3 hours or until bubbly.

1¹/₄ cups scalded milk
¹/₂ cup butter, margarine,
    or shortening
¹/₂ cup sugar
2 teaspoons salt
2 eggs, well beaten
1 package dry yeast dissolved in
    ¹/₄ cup warm water
6 to 6¹/₂ cups flour
¹/₂ cup sugar
2 tablespoons cinnamon
1 cup raisins

Heat milk to bubbly stage and add butter, margarine, or shortening, ¹/₂ cup sugar, and salt. Add beaten eggs to starter in bowl. Add yeast, then gradually add the flour and the milk mixture, beating well after each addition. Stir in enough flour to make a soft dough that is easy to handle. Allow to rest for 10 minutes. Knead on a lightly floured board until smooth and elastic. Place in a greased bowl, cover with a damp cloth, and set in a warm place to double in bulk. Punch down and allow to rest for 10 minutes. Divide in half. Roll each half into a rectangle about 10 x 18 inches and ½-inch thick. Brush with melted margarine. Sprinkle each half with a mixture of ¼ cup sugar, 1 tablespoon cinnamon, and ½ cup raisins. Roll dough as for cinnamon rolls (pp. 89–90) and seal edges tightly by pinching dough together. Shape into a ring on a greased baking sheet or 9-inch pie pan. Cut with scissors about ¾ through and approximately 1½ inches apart. Set in a warm place covered with a damp cloth and let rise until doubled. Bake at 350° for about 30 to 35 minutes, or until golden brown. Remove from pan onto a rack to cool. When cool, frost. Nuts or coconut may be added to the filling. Also, chopped dates or currants may be added or used in place of the raisins.

FROSTING FOR ELVERA'S SWEDISH
SOURDOUGH COFFEE RING:

¼ cup soft butter or margarine
2½ cups powdered sugar
2 tablespoons milk
¾ teaspoon vanilla
Chopped nuts (optional)
Candied cherries (optional)

Beat ingredients (except optionals) until smooth and creamy. Spread frosting; sprinkle coffee ring with chopped nuts and decorate with candied cherries, if desired.

Elvera's Basic Sourdough Sweet Roll Dough

1 cup sourdough starter
  (see p. 84)
1 cup warm water

1 ½ cups flour
1 cup milk
½ cup butter or margarine
¾ cup sugar
2 ½ teaspoons salt
½ teaspoon baking soda
1 package dry yeast dissolved
   in ¼ cup warm water
2 beaten eggs
5 ½ to 6 cups flour

Place starter in a large bowl. Add water and flour alternately; beat well. Return 1 cup starter to the sourdough pot, set both in a warm place, and cover with a damp cloth. Allow to rise 2 or 3 hours or overnight.

Scald milk and add butter or margarine, sugar, salt, and baking soda. To the sourdough mixture, add dry yeast dissolved in water and eggs, then add this mixture to the milk mixture alternately with about 2 ½ to 3 ½ cups flour. Continue to add more flour until dough is easy to handle, about 2 or 3 more cups. Allow to rest 10 minutes. Knead on a lightly floured board until smooth and elastic. Place in a greased bowl in a warm place until doubled in bulk. Punch down and divide dough into 2 pieces. Shape as desired for Elvera's Sourdough Cinnamon Rolls and Caramel Cinnamon Rolls on the following pages.

Elvera's Sourdough Cinnamon Rolls

Roll Elvera's Basic Sourdough Sweet Roll Dough (see pp. 88–89) into a rectangle 9 x 15 inches. Spread with 2 tablespoons melted butter or margarine and sprinkle with a mixture of ¼ cup sugar and 1 teaspoon cinnamon. Roll tightly and seal. Cut in 1 ½-inch pieces and place ¼ inch apart in a greased pan. Cover and let rise in a warm place until doubled. Bake at 375° for 25 minutes. When cool, frost with Powdered Sugar Icing. *Makes 24 rolls.*

Powdered Sugar Icing

1 cup sifted powdered sugar
1 tablespoon butter or margarine, melted
1 tablespoon milk
1/4 teaspoon vanilla

Mix all ingredients together. Stir well.

Elvera's Date-Nut-Filled Coffee Ring

1 pound dates, chopped
1/2 cup brown sugar
1/2 cup water
1/2 cup finely chopped walnuts
3 tablespoons soft butter or margarine

Cook dates, brown sugar, water, and walnuts slowly, stirring often, until mixture is soft and spreadable. Cool.

Make Elvera's Basic Sweet Roll Dough (pp. 88–89). Divide in half and roll into a rectangle about 9 × 15 inches. Brush with 3 tablespoons soft butter or margarine and spread with the date mixture. Roll up tightly and seal. Form into coffee ring with sealed edge down. Cut with scissors halfway through at about 1-inch intervals. Place ring in a greased 9-inch pie pan and let rise in warm place until doubled in bulk. Bake at 375° for 25 minutes. When cool, frost with Powdered Sugar Icing (see p. 90). *Serves 8.*

Elvera's Sourdough Caramel Cinnamon Rolls

¼ cup light corn syrup
¾ cup brown sugar
2 tablespoons butter or margarine
1 tablespoon cream

Combine ingredients, warm on low heat, and spread on bottom of pan (10 x 13 inches). Make cinnamon rolls from Elvera's Basic Sourdough Sweet Roll Dough recipe (see pp. 88–89) and place ¼ inch apart in pan. Bake at 375° for 25 minutes. Turn out of pan immediately. *Makes 24 rolls.*

Elvera's Sourdough Raised Doughnuts

The night before making doughnuts, add ¾ cup flour and ½ cup warm water to ½ cup sourdough starter (see p. 84). The next morning stir the starter down, measure out ½ cup, and return to the sourdough pot. Except for the oil and optional sugars, mix together and add to the sourdough starter:

½ cup scalded milk, cooled to lukewarm
¼ cup sugar
1 teaspoon salt
1 egg
¼ cup soft vegetable shortening
1 package dry yeast dissolved in
   2 tablespoons warm water

2¹/₂ to 3 cups flour or enough so
   dough is easy to handle
Oil for deep frying
Sugar (optional)
Powdered sugar (optional)

Knead on floured board until dough is elastic, about 5 minutes. Place in a greased bowl and allow to rise in warm place until doubled. Punch down lightly and roll out on floured board to about ¹/₂-inch thickness. Cut with 3-inch doughnut cutter and allow to rise on board until very light. Heat 3 to 4 inches oil to 375° in deep pan and drop doughnuts in, two or three at a time, and cook until brown on both sides. Drain on paper towels. When cool, sprinkle sugar on top or glaze with a mixture of ¹/₃ cup hot water and 1 cup powdered sugar, well blended. *Makes 12 doughnuts.*

PAUL CROY'S SAND-HOLE BISCUITS

*P*aul Croy lives in a beautiful log house that he and his wife, Betty, built with their own hands on a mountain overlooking Lake Pend Oreille. Paul is in his eighties now, but nearly every day still fishes the river that flows past my cabin. (I fish the river almost every day, too, but Paul actually catches fish.) He is a poet. For a Christmas present when I was about fifteen, my mother gave me a copy of Paul's first book of poems, *Old Blazes.* Like any other fifteen-year-old boy given a book of poems for Christmas, I could scarcely rein in my unbridled joy. Indeed, such was my surprise at the gift that I must have sat in silence for a full minute staring at it, my hands trembling ever so slightly as I squished the covers together. What was even more surprising is that I came to love that book of poems. Indeed, it sparked my first interest in becoming a writer myself. Paul at the time taught at Sandpoint High School, and I happened to be one of his students or, at least, to be more accurate, occupied a desk in his classroom. Academically, Paul fondly remembers me as a space in the back row that wasn't empty, except during hunting season. If there is such a thing as an Idaho Renaissance man, Paul is it: woodsman, packer, poet, writer, naturalist, sportsman, builder, teacher, and teller of tales both tall and true. I couldn't let this book go to press without including one of Paul Croy's recipes, in his own words:

"I remember an actual occurrence back in my third decade—I am now in my eighth—which I think should fill your request for an old-time recipe. A young couple who were good friends of ours stopped at our place one Friday evening to spend the weekend. After breakfast Saturday, we all agreed that it would be fun to take our fishing gear and camp outfit and take a boat ride to the mouth of the South Fork to fish and camp and come back Sunday afternoon. We loaded everything into our old sixteen-foot boat and got the motor started—Oh, I forgot, this is just a recipe. Anyway, that evening everybody wanted sourdough biscuits. I got the starter jug from the food box and discovered that we had nothing to use for a mixing bowl. So here is the recipe:

"Dig one hole in sand, about two-gallon capacity. Place rain slicker over hole, outside up. Press slicker into hole. Pour one quart starter into hole. Add one can condensed milk and one cup water. Beat two eggs in tin cup, with two tablespoons sugar. Dump in hole. Add flour and stir until dough is thick and sticky. (Oh, I forgot! You should have started your campfire about an hour ago so you have a good bed of coals by now.) Empty grub box, which is a wooden apple box, and put biscuit-size globs of dough on the side of the box. Press them to an inch thick. Now brace the box up with some driftwood so the biscuits are facing the coals. Rotate box so biscuits brown evenly. When biscuits fall off box they are done."

SALADS, SALAD DRESSINGS, AND SOUPS

Devilish Eggs

Deviled eggs were always on our picnic menu.

6 hard-boiled eggs
4 tablespoons mayonnaise
½ teaspoon prepared mustard
½ teaspoon Worcestershire sauce
1 teaspoon cider vinegar
Salt and pepper to taste
Paprika
Celery, onion, pickles, relish, olives (optional)

Shell eggs and cut in half lengthwise; remove yolks. Mash yolks; add mayonnaise and seasonings. Finely minced celery, onion, pickles, relish, or olives can be added to yolks at this time. Pile mixture into egg-white halves and sprinkle with paprika. Refrigerate until ready to serve. *Serves 6.*

Frozen Cherry Salad

2 (3-ounce)packages cream cheese
½ cup mayonnaise
¼ cup sugar
1 tablespoon lemon juice
1 cup miniature marshmallows
1 pint canned Bing cherries,
   well drained and pitted
1 can (8 ounces) crushed pineapple,
   well drained
1 cup whipping cream

Using a mixer, beat together cream cheese, mayonnaise, sugar, and lemon juice. Fold in marshmallows, cherries, and crushed pineapple. Whip cream and fold into above mixture. Pour into mold and freeze. *Serves 6.*

Tipsy Fresh-Fruit Salad

2 quarts fruit
Allspice
Honey
Vodka

Choose any fairly solid fresh fruit or berry available, such as watermelon balls, cantaloupe balls, seedless grapes, pineapple chunks, sliced bananas, orange sections, sliced apples, cherries, sliced pears, strawberries, blueberries. Sprinkle sparingly with allspice. Mix honey and vodka together (1 part vodka to 3 parts honey). Pour over salad. Toss gently and serve immediately. *Serves 8.*

Six-Cup Salad

    1 cup pineapple tidbits, drained
    1 cup mandarin oranges, drained
    1 cup sliced bananas
    1 cup miniature marshmallows
    1 cup coconut
    1 cup sour cream

Combine ingredients and toss lightly. Chill. *Serves 6.*

Mom's Waldorf Salad

    4 medium red apples, chopped,
       with peeling left on
    1 cup diced celery
    1/2 cup chopped walnuts
    1/2 cup mayonnaise

Mix above ingredients together. *Serves 4.*

Winter Fruit Salad

This salad will keep for several days in the refrigerator.

1/4 cup mayonnaise
1 pint cream-style cottage cheese
1/2 teaspoon salt
1/2 teaspoon dry mustard
1/2 pint cream, whipped with 3 tablespoons sugar
1 can (16 ounces) fruit cocktail, drained
1 can (8 ounces) pineapple chunks, drained
1 can (11 ounces) mandarin oranges, drained
1 cup miniature marshmallows

Gently stir mayonnaise into cottage cheese. Add salt and dry mustard; fold in whipped cream. Add well-drained fruit and marshmallows and combine. Chill for several hours. *Serves 8.*

Hellroaring Three-Bean Salad

1 can (15 ounces) green beans, drained
1 can (15 ounces) red kidney beans, drained
1 can (15 ounces) garbanzo beans, drained
1/2 onion, chopped
1/2 green pepper, chopped (optional)
1/4 cup minced fresh parsley
1/2 cup cider vinegar
1 cup salad oil
1/2 cup sugar
Pinch of salt
2 cloves garlic

Mix vegetables and parsley together. Make dressing with vinegar, salad oil, sugar, salt, and garlic. Pour over vegetables. Cover and refrigerate for at least 3 hours. Remove garlic before serving. *Serves 12.*

Coleslaw

1 large head green cabbage, shredded
   (about 2 quarts)
1 green bell pepper, diced (optional)
1 large onion, diced
1 carrot, grated (optional)
1 cup sugar
1 teaspoon salt
1/2 teaspoon pepper
1 tablespoon celery seed
3/4 teaspoon dry mustard
3/4 cup salad oil
1 cup cider vinegar

Layer 1/2 shredded cabbage into a large bowl that has a tight-fitting lid. Add 1/2 diced bell pepper, 1/2 diced onion, and half grated carrot. Sprinkle with 1/2 cup sugar. Continue with another layer of cabbage, green pepper, onion, and carrot. Sprinkle with remaining 1/2 cup sugar. Bring the remaining ingredients to a boil. Remove from heat, allow to cool, and pour the mixture over the vegetables. Do not stir. Cover tightly and refrigerate for at least 4 hours, then stir. This coleslaw will keep for 3 days. *Serves 12.*

Cucumbers in Sour Cream

3 large cucumbers
1 teaspoon salt
1 cup sour cream
1/3 cup mayonnaise
1 tablespoon tarragon vinegar
2 green onions, including part of tops,
    thinly sliced
1 tablespoon fresh parsley, finely minced
1 small clove garlic, minced
1 teaspoon Worcestershire sauce

Pare cucumbers and slice very thin. Sprinkle with salt and let stand while preparing sauce. Combine remaining ingredients and mix until well blended. Drain liquid from cucumbers, pour sauce over, and blend well. Cover and refrigerate for at least 2 hours. *Serves 6 to 8.*

Onion Relish

When we had nothing to make a salad with, which was most of the time, we often had onion relish. Onions were peeled and chopped up fairly fine. We would mix vinegar, sugar, salt, and pepper to taste in a cup and pour over the onion. It was much better if it could set for a while; however, it was usually a last-minute thought. Surprisingly, it tasted great to us with our fried potatoes and eggs.

*T*he Old Woodcutter lived in a tiny cabin on the mountain behind the school at Squaw Valley. He survived almost entirely off the land. In the two years we knew him, he never once went to town. Other than the dandelion greens, I don't know how he came up with the rest of the ingredients for this salad. I suppose he borrowed them from us or the other neighbors. It's difficult to refuse a poor, ragged, lame, crazy old man who shows up at your door with a sharp, double-bitted ax over his shoulder.

Old Woodcutter's Dandelion Salad

1 pound bacon
8 eggs
2 tablespoons sugar
¼ cup cider vinegar
Salt and pepper to taste
2 quarts young dandelion greens,
    cleaned and chopped

Fry bacon crisp, remove from pan, and crumble. Pour off all but 2 tablespoons drippings; scramble the eggs in drippings, leaving them still soft. Add sugar, vinegar, bacon, salt, and pepper and stir. Add dandelion greens, and just heat through. *Serves 6.*

Gram's Wilted Dandelion Green Salad

6 cups dandelion greens, cleaned
   and chopped
3 green onions, thinly sliced
4 slices bacon, fried crisp,
   drained, and crumbled
1/4 cup cider vinegar
1/4 cup water
3 tablespoons sugar
Salt and pepper to taste
Bacon drippings

Place dandelion greens and green onions in bowl. Add crumbled bacon. Add vinegar, water, sugar, salt, and pepper to bacon drippings. Heat to boiling and pour over dandelion greens. Toss well and serve immediately. *Serves 4.*

Idaho Potato Salad

6 medium potatoes, cooked in jackets
   until tender
1 bunch green onions, finely sliced,
   including green tops
2 stalks celery, diced
1/2 cup chopped sweet pickles
1/4 cup diced pimento
5 hard-boiled eggs, chopped
Salt and pepper to taste

Gram's Homemade Salad Dressing
(see p. 106)

Cool potatoes, peel, and chop. Add rest of ingredients and mix together lightly. Moisten to desired consistency with salad dressing. *Serves 8.*

You don't find many families anymore who have a crock of sauerkraut sitting out in the woodshed. I suppose that's because most people don't have woodsheds anymore. A crock of sauerkraut isn't something you want to keep in the house, or even too near the house, unless it's downwind. A handful of kraut snatched out of the crock was a favorite after-school snack of mine, but only because there weren't any other after-school snacks available. Even though the kraut was left out in the cold woodshed all winter, it never seemed to freeze. Probably not a good sign. I think the kraut may have been spoiled, but with kraut it is difficult to tell. It always smells spoiled. In fact, spoiled may be the natural state of sauerkraut. I wasn't aware of any ill effects from snacking on the kraut out of the crock in the woodshed, but one day years later, shortly after eating some wieners and sauerkraut for lunch, I suddenly found myself teaching verbals to a class in freshman composition. It was scary, and certainly not something I would want to go through again. I haven't touched sauerkraut since.

Klaus's Sauerkraut Salad

1 can (16 ounces) sauerkraut
½ cup salad oil
1 cup cider vinegar
¾ cup sugar

1 medium onion, chopped
1 cup chopped celery
1 green pepper, chopped

Rinse sauerkraut with cold water, drain, and chop. Mix oil, vinegar, and sugar. Combine the vegetables with the sauerkraut and pour the oil mixture over. Mix well and refrigerate for 8 hours. *Serves 6.*

Tomato Salad

1 cup olive oil
⅓ cup wine vinegar
2 teaspoons dried oregano leaves,
    crushed
1 teaspoon salt
½ teaspoon pepper
½ teaspoon dry mustard
2 cloves garlic, crushed
8 to 10 thick slices peeled tomatoes
    or peeled small tomatoes
Green onions, minced
Fresh parsley, chopped

Mix all ingredients except tomatoes, onions, and parsley. Pour over tomatoes and chill for 2 or 3 hours. Drain tomatoes, reserving dressing, and place in serving dish. Sprinkle with minced green onion and parsley. Pour a little dressing over the top. This dressing can be saved and reused. *Serves 5.*

Vegetable Layered Salad

$\frac{1}{2}$ pound bacon
1 package (10 ounces) frozen peas
6 cups lettuce or other greens,
    torn into bite-size pieces
1 cup sliced green onions
1 cup diced celery
$\frac{1}{2}$ cup diced green pepper (optional)
$\frac{1}{2}$ cup sliced fresh mushrooms
2 cups shredded Cheddar cheese
1 cup mayonnaise
$\frac{3}{4}$ cup sour cream
2 tablespoons sugar

Cook bacon until crisp; drain and crumble. Pour hot water over peas in sieve just until thawed, then rinse with cold water, and drain well. Using a bowl with a tight-fitting lid, layer the lettuce, onions, celery, green pepper, peas, mushrooms, and Cheddar cheese. Mix the mayonnaise and sour cream and frost top of the salad, then sprinkle lightly with sugar. Sprinkle crumbled bacon over the top. Cover tightly and refrigerate for 10 to 12 hours. Toss before serving. *Serves 12.*

Blue Cheese Dressing

1 package (4 ounces) blue cheese, crumbled
1 package (3 ounces) cream cheese, softened
$\frac{1}{2}$ cup mayonnaise
$\frac{1}{3}$ cup light cream
2 tablespoons lemon juice

1 clove garlic, grated
3 tablespoons grated onion

Beat all ingredients until well blended. Keep refrigerated in covered container. *Makes 1²/₃ cups.*

Cowpoke Western Dressing

1 cup sugar
2 teaspoons salt
2 teaspoons paprika
Juice of 4 lemons
4 tablespoons cider vinegar
4 tablespoons Worcestershire sauce
2²/₃ cups catsup
4 cups salad oil
Minced garlic and grated onion to taste

Combine above ingredients and blend till smooth. *Makes almost 2 quarts.*

French Dressing

¹/₂ cup salad oil
³/₄ cup sugar
1 teaspoon salt
1 teaspoon paprika
²/₃ cup catsup
³/₄ cup cider vinegar
4 tablespoons fresh lemon juice

1 teaspoon garlic salt
1 teaspoon celery salt
1 large onion, grated

Combine ingredients in large bowl and beat well with mixer. *Makes about 2¹/₂ cups.*

Poppy Seed Dressing

³/₄ cup sugar
1 teaspoon dry mustard
1 teaspoon salt
¹/₃ cup cider vinegar
1¹/₂ tablespoons onion juice
1 cup salad oil
2 tablespoons poppy seeds

Combine sugar, mustard, salt, and vinegar. Add onion juice and stir thoroughly. Add oil slowly, beating constantly, and continue to beat until thick. Stir in poppy seeds. Keep refrigerated. *Makes about 2 cups.*

Gram's Homemade Salad Dressing

This dressing is particularly good for potato salad, macaroni salad, or coleslaw.

2 tablespoons flour
1 teaspoon salt
³/₄ cup sugar

1 egg, beaten
3/4 cup cider vinegar
1 tablespoon butter or margarine
1 teaspoon prepared mustard
1/4 teaspoon paprika
Mayonnaise

Combine dry ingredients, add egg, and mix well. Add vinegar and cook in double boiler over boiling water until thick, stirring constantly. When mixture has thickened, remove from heat. Add butter or margarine, mustard, and paprika. Cool and refrigerate. Combine dressing with mayonnaise to taste when ready to use. *Makes about 1½ cups (before mayonnaise).*

Pretty Darn Special
Salad Dressing

2 teaspoons salt
2 teaspoons celery seed
2 teaspoons dry mustard
2 teaspoons paprika
3/4 cup sugar
1/2 cup cider vinegar
2 tablespoons grated onion
2 cups salad oil

Mix ingredients together in top of double boiler and stir well. Place over warm water and continue stirring until ingredients are lukewarm. Remove from double boiler and beat until slightly thick and blended. Refrigerate. *Makes 3 cups.*

Thousand Island Dressing

1 cup mayonnaise
2 tablespoons catsup
2 tablespoons sweet pickle relish,
   well drained
⅓ cup diced celery
¼ cup minced onion
1 tablespoon pimento, diced
2 tablespoons fresh minced parsley
1 tablespoon lemon juice
Salt and pepper to taste

Combine ingredients gently and keep refrigerated until ready
to use. *Makes about 2 cups.*

Southern Idaho Basque Soup

1 pound ground beef
1 large jar spaghetti sauce (32 ounces) or
   4 cups homemade spaghetti sauce
1 pint canned tomatoes
1 can (6 ounces) tomato sauce
1 can (16 ounces) garbanzo beans and juice
1 can (6 ounces) black olives, drained
5 cloves fresh garlic, sliced
10 fresh mushrooms, sliced
1 cup diced celery
1 cup diced onion
1½ cups diced carrots
1 cup Italian green beans, fresh or canned
1 pint water

1 yam or white potato, diced
1 cup red wine (optional)
Salt, pepper, and paprika

Combine all ingredients and simmer until tender. Season to taste with salt, pepper, and paprika. *Serves 12.*

Bean Soup

1 cup navy beans
1 quart water
1 ham bone with some ham left on it
1 medium onion, chopped
3 carrots, diced
3 stalks celery, diced
Salt and pepper to taste
$1/4$ teaspoon prepared mustard
$1/2$ bay leaf
1 clove garlic, minced

Wash beans, cover with water, and soak overnight. Drain, but retain water. Place all ingredients in kettle and simmer approximately 3 hours or until beans are cooked. Cut ham from bone, dice, and return to soup. Adjust seasonings. Add more water to soup as needed. *Serves 6.*

Mrs. Sweeney's Cream of Chicken and Carrot Soup

2 pounds bony chicken pieces
6 cups water

$\frac{1}{2}$ cup chopped onion
$\frac{1}{2}$ cup chopped celery
$\frac{1}{4}$ cup butter or margarine
6 large carrots, chopped
1 cup whipping cream
2 tablespoons minced fresh parsley
Salt and pepper to taste

Simmer chicken pieces in enough water to cover them, until tender. Save broth and strain. Skin and bone chicken and chop meat into small pieces. Sauté onion and celery in butter or margarine until tender. Add onion, celery, and carrots to 5 cups broth and cook until carrots are tender. Strain vegetables from broth and puree or mash well. Return vegetables and chopped chicken to broth. Add cream and parsley. Salt and pepper to taste. Reheat, but do not boil. *Serves 8.*

Clam Chowder

4 slices bacon, cut in $\frac{1}{2}$-inch pieces
1 large onion, minced
3 potatoes, chopped
2 cups chicken broth
2 cups light cream
2 ($6\frac{1}{2}$-ounce) cans minced clams
Salt and pepper to taste
2 tablespoons dried dill weed

Sauté bacon until crisp and remove from pan. Discard all but 3 tablespoons bacon grease. Place onion and potatoes in pan with bacon grease and sauté until tender, but not brown. Add the chicken broth. Cook over low heat until vegetables are soft. Add the cream and minced clams. Cook over very low heat until chowder is slightly thickened, but do not allow to boil. Season to taste with salt and pepper. Add dill weed and crumbled bacon. *Serves 6.*

Corn Chowder

¼ pound bacon
2 potatoes, chopped
½ medium onion, chopped
1 can (17 ounces) cream-style corn
3 cups milk
Salt and pepper to taste

Fry bacon until crisp. Remove from pan and crumble. Remove all but 2 tablespoons bacon grease from pan. Add potatoes and onion and sauté until soft but not brown. Add corn and milk; simmer for a few minutes. Season to taste with salt and pepper. *Serves 6.*

Gram's Leftover Fish Chowder

4 slices bacon
3 tablespoons bacon grease or margarine
1 onion, diced

½ cup diced celery
¼ cup diced green pepper (optional)
3 potatoes, diced
2 cups chicken broth
1 tablespoon minced fresh parsley
1 teaspoon dried dill weed
2 cups light cream
3 to 4 cups cooked fish (or 1 pint
   canned kokanee)
Salt and pepper to taste

Fry bacon until crisp. Remove from pan and crumble. Remove all but 3 tablespoons bacon grease from pan and sauté onion, celery, and green pepper until tender. Add potatoes, chicken broth, parsley, and dill weed. Simmer until potatoes are tender. Add light cream and fish. Season to taste with salt and pepper. Reheat, but do not boil. Pour into bowls and sprinkle crumbled bacon over top. *Serves 6.*

I am not fond of lentil soup, or of lentils in any other form, if they even have another form. (Lentil-flavored ice cream?) It is disloyal and unpatriotic of me to admit this, because Moscow, Idaho, claims to be "The Lentil Capital of the World." There are so many other things that Moscow has to be proud of, and it chooses to be "Lentil Capital of the World." Give me a break! My old kid-camping buddy Norm Nelson lives there. Why couldn't Moscow put up a sign saying "Home of Norm Nelson"? Moscow has a fine university and could proclaim itself "The Home of the University of Idaho." It has a dozen other distinctive and admirable characteristics, not least of which is being One of the World's Friendliest Towns. But it picks the lentil for its motto, its mark of distinction. This is a tourist attraction? "Wake up, kids! We're almost to the Lentil Capital of the World!"

"Gee, Dad, can I get a lentil T-shirt?"

"You betcha, son. We didn't drive two thousand miles to see the Lentil Capital of the World without buying a bunch of lentil souvenirs. We're going to eat in the Lentil Restaurant, stay at the Lentil Resort, and go on all the lentil rides, too."

"Wow! What's a lentil, anyway, Dad?"

"Beats the heck out of me, son."

I must admit that the rest of my family loves lentil soup. As I always say, there's no accounting for taste.

Lentil Soup

Any smoked sausage is delicious in this soup. If you don't have sausage, use ³/₄ pound cooked bacon.

2 cups lentils
¹/₂ pound Kielbasa sausage, coarsely chopped,
   or ³/₄ pound cooked bacon
1 large onion, chopped
3 stalks celery, chopped
3 carrots, chopped
2 quarts water
1 clove garlic, minced
1 bay leaf
¹/₂ teaspoon thyme
1 tablespoon dried dill weed
Salt and pepper to taste

Wash lentils and drain. Mix all ingredients except dill weed. Cover and simmer until lentils are soft. Add dill weed. Correct seasonings and simmer an additional half hour. *Serves 10.*

Mom's Potato Soup

4 potatoes, peeled and chopped
2 cups boiling water
1/4 pound bacon with grease retained
1 onion, chopped
1 quart milk
1 tablespoon dried parsley, crushed
2 tablespoons butter or margarine
Salt and pepper to taste

Cook potatoes in boiling water until soft. Drain. Remove half of the potatoes and mash. Fry bacon until crisp. Remove from pan and crumble. Sauté onion in 3 tablespoons bacon grease. Heat milk and add chopped potatoes, onion, bacon, parsley, and butter or margarine. Stir in mashed potatoes. Salt and pepper to taste. *Serves 4.*

Split Pea Soup

2 1/4 cups green split peas
6 cups water
1 meaty ham bone
1 cup onion, chopped
1 cup celery, diced
1 cup carrots, diced
1/4 teaspoon marjoram
1/2 bay leaf
Salt, pepper, and garlic powder to taste
2 cups milk

Wash peas thoroughly. Combine all ingredients except milk. Simmer for 1 hour, stirring occasionally, or until peas and vegetables are soft. Remove ham bone. Cut away the meat and dice it. Return meat to soup. Add milk. Correct seasonings and simmer 20 minutes longer. *Serves 8.*

Skookum Minestrone Soup

This soup is wonderful to serve to a crowd of hungry people—especially on a cold, wet day.

1 pound ground venison or beef
3 tablespoons vegetable shortening
1 quart water
1 can (28 ounces) tomatoes
1 large onion, chopped
2 large carrots, peeled and sliced
2 (8-ounce) cans tomato sauce
2 cups beef broth
1 tablespoon dried parsley, crushed
$^{1}/_{2}$ teaspoon dried basil, crushed
1 teaspoon dried oregano, crushed
$^{1}/_{2}$ teaspoon pepper
$1^{1}/_{2}$ teaspoons salt
$^{1}/_{2}$ teaspoon garlic salt
1 can (15 ounces) garbanzo beans, drained
1 can (16 ounces) green beans, drained
1 can (15 ounces) kidney beans, drained
$1^{1}/_{4}$ cups uncooked macaroni
Parmesan cheese (optional)

Brown venison or beef in shortening. Combine all ingredients except Parmesan cheese and bring to a boil. Cover and simmer over low heat about 40 minutes. Garnish each bowl of soup with Parmesan cheese, if desired. *Serves 12.*

Mom's Homemade Tomato Soup

We had this soup for lunch or dinner several times a week—the one reason Mom canned tomatoes. When we complained, Mom would add cooked rice or something worse to it. We soon learned to keep quiet about her tomato soup.

1 pint home-canned tomatoes
$1/2$ teaspoon baking soda
3 cups milk, heated
3 tablespoons butter or margarine
Salt and pepper to taste

Chop tomatoes into small pieces. If not enough juice, add $1/4$ cup water. Bring to boil and add baking soda. Remove from heat, cool slightly, and add milk. Add butter or margarine, salt and pepper to taste. *Serves 4.*

Turkey Carcass Noodle Soup

1 turkey carcass
8 cups water
1 large chopped onion
1 cup celery, chopped
1 carrot, chopped
1 pint tomatoes
1 clove garlic, minced

¼ cup chopped fresh parsley
½ bay leaf
Salt and pepper to taste
Aunt Verda's Noodles (see p. 67)

Place carcass and water in large pot. Simmer for 2 hours. Remove carcass from pot and strip meat from bones. Chop well and return to pot. Add vegetables, garlic, parsley, bay leaf, salt, and pepper. Simmer until vegetables are tender. Raise heat slightly and add the amount of noodles needed, being sure there is plenty of liquid in pot. Cook until noodles are tender. If possible, use homemade noodles. *Serves 6.*

VEGETABLES AND CASSEROLES

Three-Bean Casserole

    ½ pound hamburger
    ¼ pound Italian sausage
    ½ cup chopped bacon with grease retained
    1 medium onion, chopped
    1 can (15 ounces) kidney beans, drained
    1 can (15 ounces) pork and beans
    1 can (15 ounces) lima beans, drained
    ⅓ cup white sugar
    ⅓ cup packed brown sugar
    ¼ cup barbecue sauce
    ¼ cup catsup
    1 tablespoon prepared mustard
    ½ to 1 tablespoon chili powder

Fry hamburger and sausage in skillet, stirring to separate until brown. Drain and remove to casserole dish. Fry bacon until crisp, chop, and add to casserole. Add onion to 3 tablespoons bacon fat and sauté until tender. Drain off fat. Combine beans, hamburger, sausage, bacon, and onion. Stir remaining ingredients together and stir into beans. Pour into casserole and bake for 1 hour at 350°. *Serves 12.*

Creamed Cabbage

We often had this for supper served over mashed potatoes.

2 cups water
1 teaspoon salt
1 small onion, chopped
½ medium head cabbage, shredded
1 egg
1 cup light cream
2 tablespoons butter or margarine

Place first 3 ingredients in kettle and let cook while you shred the cabbage. Add cabbage and cook until tender. Drain off water. Beat egg and cream with fork and add slowly to the cabbage. Stir in butter or margarine. Do not boil. *Serves 4.*

Fried Cabbage

2 tablespoons salad oil
2 tablespoons butter or margarine
1 medium head cabbage, shredded coarsely
1 teaspoon sugar
Salt and pepper to taste
½ teaspoon caraway seeds

Heat oil and butter or margarine in large heavy skillet. Add cabbage and stir over medium-high heat. Sprinkle with sugar; add salt and pepper to taste. Cook until tender-crisp. Sprinkle with caraway seeds. *Serves 4.*

Stuffed Cabbage Rolls

1 large head cabbage
1½ pounds ground venison or elk
1 cup cooked rice
1 medium onion, diced
2 eggs, beaten
½ teaspoon celery salt
½ teaspoon salt
Dash of pepper

Steam cabbage until outer leaves wilt. Carefully remove 16 large outer leaves and cut away heavy rib in center. Combine remaining ingredients and shape into 16 balls. Place ball of stuffing inside each leaf, turn sides in, and roll so that stuffing is completely covered. Tie each leaf with string. Simmer for 1 hour in sauce. *Serves 8.*

SAUCE:

¼ cup cider vinegar
½ cup packed brown sugar
1 can (8 ounces) tomato sauce
1 can beer (or enough to cover cabbage rolls)

Combine sauce ingredients and heat to simmering.

Gram's Sweet-and-Sour Red Cabbage

6 slices bacon
1 medium onion, chopped
6 cups red cabbage, shredded
$\frac{1}{2}$ cup water
Salt and pepper to taste
2 cups peeled apples, thinly sliced
$\frac{1}{2}$ cup cider vinegar
$\frac{1}{4}$ cup packed brown sugar

Cook bacon in large skillet until crisp. Remove from drippings and set aside. Remove all but 2 tablespoons drippings, add onion, and cook until tender-crisp. Add cabbage, water, and salt and pepper to taste. Cover and cook over low heat for about 10 minutes. Add apples, vinegar, and brown sugar. Cover and cook 10 to 15 minutes longer, or until apples are tender and liquid is absorbed. Crumble bacon over cabbage. *Serves 6.*

Corn Pudding

2 tablespoons butter or margarine
2 tablespoons flour
3 tablespoons sugar
1 can ($14\frac{1}{2}$ ounces) evaporated milk
1 can (16 ounces) cream-style corn
2 eggs, well beaten
Salt and pepper to taste

Melt butter or margarine; add flour and sugar. Stir in milk and corn. Add eggs, salt and pepper to taste. Put in greased casserole dish and set in pan of hot water. Bake at 350° for 1 hour or until knife inserted in center comes out clean. *Serves 6.*

Baked Carrots

12 large carrots, peeled and sliced
1/2 cup butter or margarine
1/2 cup packed brown sugar
1/2 teaspoon baking powder
2 eggs, beaten
1 cup evaporated milk
Salt and pepper to taste
Approximately 1/4 cup fine bread crumbs

Cook peeled and sliced carrots; drain. Add butter or margarine and mash. Stir in remaining ingredients, except bread crumbs, and beat lightly. Pour into greased casserole. Sprinkle bread crumbs on top and bake at 350° for 30 minutes. *Serves 8.*

GRAM'S GREENS

*F*ew things filled me with more dread than the sight of my grandmother coming through the door with a basket of wild greens. If wild greens were actually good, they would be sold in grocery stores for big prices. That was my theory then, and it is my theory now. Still, I know many people who pick and eat wild greens and find them good. My wife, Bun, is one of these people. She is a wild-food expert. "Look," she will say on one of our little outings, "wild burdock. That's good to eat."

"No it isn't," I say.

She digs out one of her wild-food books and points to the illustration of burdock. "See right here. It says edible."

"Edible doesn't mean good," I riposte. "Edible only means it won't kill you. I don't consider the claim that something won't kill me to be a great recommendation."

I personally don't eat weeds, but Bun frequently orders me onto a vacant lot to pull some. So I'm standing there tugging on a big weed, and the guy who owns the lot shows up. He is big and brawny with a jaw like an anvil. This is the first time he has visited his vacant lot in nine years, and I, a total stranger, have to be standing there abusing one of his weeds.

"Uh," I say, "I hope you don't mind if I pull your burdock."

Right away I see the guy doesn't know his edible weeds. That is one reason picking wild greens can be so risky—ignorance.

Speaking of ignorance, I remember the time the old woodsman Rancid Crabtree picked a couple of leaves from a plant and handed me one of them. "Ever eat miner's lettuce?" he asked. We each chewed on the stringy leaves for a second or two. "Wahl, this ain't it!" he cried, green foam dribbling down his chin. "Now let this be a good lesson to you!" Fortunately, the plant wasn't life-threatening, if you don't count a kid and an old woodsman nearly trampling each other to death on the way to the nearest water. Even after we washed our mouths out with a couple of gallons of spring water, I thought they would be permanently puckered. I asked Rancid how long he thought the puckering might last. "Ooo dah 'ell dooo Ahh knewww?" he replied.

I must admit that there are some people who enjoy wild greens, and I probably could learn to like them myself. On the other hand, there are more pleasant things to learn, such as ancient Greek or quantum theory.

Boiled Dandelion Greens

Gather only the tender, young leaves, because as the plant ages, the leaves become bitter.

Dandelion greens
Butter or margarine
Salt and pepper
Cider vinegar

Wash young dandelion greens thoroughly, changing water 3 or 4 times. Place in saucepan and cover with boiling water. Cook until tender, 12 to 15 minutes. Drain well and chop fine. Place in frying pan with melted butter or margarine, season with salt and pepper, and stir until hot. Serve with vinegar and more melted butter or margarine.

Dandelions in Cheese Sauce

1/2 cup water
1/2 teaspoon salt
8 cups young dandelion greens
1/4 cup butter or margarine
1/4 cup flour
1 teaspoon salt
1/4 teaspoon pepper
1/2 teaspoon dry mustard
2 cups milk
2 cups grated medium-sharp Cheddar cheese
1 small can sliced mushrooms, drained

Bring salted water to a boil, add dandelion greens, and cook for 12 to 15 minutes until greens are tender. Drain. Melt butter or margarine in saucepan; add flour, 1 teaspoon salt, pepper, and mustard, stirring until smooth. Add milk gradually, in small increments, stirring constantly. Bring to boil, reduce heat, and simmer for 1 minute or until thickened. Add grated cheese and stir until cheese is melted. Add dandelion greens and mushrooms. Heat. *Serves 6.*

Fiddlehead Ferns

Fiddlehead ferns are generally found near streams where the soil is rich, although we have found them growing under the porch of our house. Pick only the fiddleheads that are still tightly furled and covered with brown scales. Soak them in cold water to clean them and rub off the scales. Soak again. You can eat them raw or cooked. To cook, bring ½-inch water to simmering stage, add fiddleheads, and simmer until tender-crisp, 7 or 8 minutes. Drain, pour melted butter over them, and add salt and pepper to taste. Fiddlehead ferns taste much like fresh asparagus. The cooked fiddleheads can also be added to soups, casseroles, or salads.

Stinging Nettles

We had almost an acre of stinging nettles in our cow pasture; even the cows had sense enough to stay away from them. We came in contact with the nettles so often—always painful contact—that we had a healthy respect for them, enough to give them a wide berth when we were herding cows. However, some fool friend of Pat's told Gram how delicious they were cooked. Nothing would do but she had to have some to try. We had to pick them. We put on gloves but didn't think about our faces, arms, and legs. Every time we picked a leaf we were stabbed by a nettle.

There is a reason for calling them "stinging nettles." But if someone else can pick your nettles for you, they are very delicious.

4 slices bacon
1/2 teaspoon salt
3 tablespoons sugar
Water (enough to boil nettles in)
3 quarts stinging nettles
3 tablespoons butter or margarine
Cider vinegar
Salt and pepper to taste

Fry bacon until crisp, and crumble. Set aside. Add salt and sugar to water and bring to boil. Add nettles to water very carefully. Cook until they are tender; drain well. Add butter or margarine, a few sprinkles of vinegar, salt and pepper to taste, and crumbled bacon. Toss and serve. *Serves 4.*

MOREL MUSHROOMS

*S*end the children from the room. We are about to discuss wild passionate love here, no holds barred.

I'm going to tell you about my mistress, with whom I've carried on a love affair for over fifty years. As mistresses go, this one is a little homely, at least until you get to know her intimately. She is about the size, shape, and color of a thumb smacked with a hammer and left untreated, kind of blackish-brown and badly wrinkled all over. I am speaking, of course, of the morel mushroom.

I have picked thousands of morels, and they have never been enough. I have known people who would practically kill to find a good patch of morels. Such behavior is extreme and unwarranted, however, particularly since breaking a leg or an arm or extracting fingernails with pliers will often motivate the subject to divulge his secret morel patch. If not, serious measures may have to be resorted to. The CIA could take lessons in secrecy from dedicated morel hunters.

I started picking wild mushrooms when I was five years old and have been at it ever since. All the members of my family were wild about wild mushrooms, particularly the morel. We picked and ate several varieties, including some I later learned were toxic. I don't eat the toxic mushrooms anymore, although the Troll still does. I suppose I should tell her one of these days.

It is not a good idea to start picking any wild mushrooms, let alone eating them, without some expert instruction first. I am not going to offer any such instruction here, because you might take my advice, then accidentally eat the wrong kind of mushroom, and shortly thereafter believe yourself to be a green chicken tap-dancing naked in a display window of a department store. Or you might be dead, one of the less desirable side effects of eating the wrong wild mushroom and quite likely to ruin your day. Then whom would you blame? Right.

The morel is one of the safer wild mushrooms to pick, because its distinctive cone shape, coloring, and texture are not duplicated by any poisonous mushroom, at least none I am familiar with.

The pleasure of morels comes not only in the eating but also in the hunting of them. They are a spring mushroom for

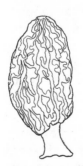

the most part, although I have occasionally found them after a summer rain. Years ago, when I found a patch of dried-up morels, I would pass them by. Then my wife started preserving mushrooms by drying them, a little trick she learned from watching squirrels. (Any day now I expect also to see her scampering overhead on telephone wires, but so far that hasn't happened.) Now I pick any dried morels I find and then reconstitute them in water, just like any other dried mushroom. It's a good idea to soak wild mushrooms in salt water to evict any small beings who may have taken up residence there. During this process, the dried mushrooms will reconstitute and be scarcely distinguishable from the fresh ones. As an extra precaution, Bun cuts through all wild mushrooms lengthwise to check out the identifying features of the internal structure before cooking them up for dinner.

As with most wild foods, many kinds of mushrooms are classified in field guides as "edible," but that doesn't mean they are good. I have sampled perhaps a dozen different species of "edible" mushrooms and found most of them okay. In my opinion, merely okay is not worth the trouble and, particularly, not worth the risk of messing around with something that is potentially lethal. That is why I concentrate my mushrooming on the morel, which is great, and a couple of other kinds that are excellent but a bit riskier.

You can't be too careful when dealing with wild mushrooms. In my distant youth, I hung around with the old woodsman Rancid Crabtree, who picked all sorts of mushrooms, dried them, and stored them in a crock. Whenever he wanted mushroom soup, he grabbed a couple of handfuls of them and boiled them in a pot of water. One day he offered to share his soup with me. I declined the invitation. Fifty-seven years later he died. So there you are. Some people are just darned lucky.

Hunting morels is as much fun as hunting anything else. Observing nature is all right, and I enjoy it, but the problem with observing something is that you're over here and the thing being observed is over there. You are never directly involved with it, never part of it. That is the appeal of hunting. You become a player in the real game of nature. You are no longer merely a spectator up in the bleachers. You may be a person who doesn't like the idea of packing a rifle or a shotgun and taking it into the woods, but you can still enjoy the essence of hunting in your search for wild mushrooms or wild berries or any other wild food, for that matter. I get the same pleasure from tracking down a covey of morels as I do hunting larger and faster game. A morel mushroom is about as small and slow a target as you're likely to bag, but no less difficult to hunt. For example, you seldom find a deer hiding under a cottonwood leaf. If you did, you would have no trouble knowing it was there. Morel hunters will walk along studying the leaf carpet of the previous fall, knowing that a leaf bulging up from the carpet may have been dislodged by a newly hatched morel beneath it. They will search for the same kinds of vegetation associated with other morels they have found. They will study trees, knowing that a particular stage of leaf development usually occurs simultaneously with the arrival of morels in the spring. The morel hunter becomes intimately involved with the habits and habitats of his quarry, as does the deer hunter with his. The mushroomer's visual perception may be honed to an even finer edge than the big-game hunter's. I know hunters who take great pride in being able to spot the antlers of a buck deer protruding above a log a quarter of a mile away. That's nothing. I can be driving down the highway at sixty miles an hour with Bun, and she will suddenly shout, "Stop the car! I just spotted a morel under some pine needles behind that grove of trees!" Now that's perception. On the other hand, Bun's morel is sometimes a pinecone. Like the true hunter, she will never admit she made a mistake. "Well, there most certainly was a morel here. You must have spooked it when you came clomping up."

Creamed Onions

This is a Thanksgiving must in our house!

8 white onions (golf-ball size)
2 tablespoons butter or margarine
2 tablespoons flour
$1/2$ teaspoon salt
$1/8$ teaspoon white pepper
$1/4$ teaspoon dry mustard

1 cup milk
Paprika

Simmer onions until just tender, and drain. Melt butter or margarine in saucepan; stir in flour and seasonings. Cook over low heat, allowing to boil 1 minute. Remove from heat and add milk. Return to heat and cook, stirring until thickened. Add onions and continue cooking until onions are heated through. Sprinkle with paprika. *Serves 4.*

Colcannon

Colcannon, an Irish dish, was served for dinner 2 or 3 times a week. If there was no cabbage or carrots, another root vegetable was substituted. A supply of root vegetables and cabbage was stocked in the root cellar in late fall because they kept so well during the winter.

6 medium potatoes, peeled
1 medium onion, finely chopped
½ small head cabbage, shredded
¼ cup water
Pinch of salt
⅓ to ½ cup milk
⅓ cup butter or margarine, softened
Salt and pepper to taste

Boil potatoes until tender and drain. Cook onion and cabbage in ¼ cup water with pinch of salt added, until tender-crisp, 5 to 6 minutes. Drain. Mash potatoes until smooth. Beat in milk in small amounts. Add butter or margarine and salt and pepper to taste. Beat until potatoes are light and fluffy. Fold in cabbage and onions. Pour in dish and dot with butter or margarine. *Serves 6.*

Boxty-in-the-Pan

1 cup grated raw potatoes
1 cup flour
2 teaspoons baking powder
2 teaspoons salt
1 cup mashed potatoes
2 eggs, beaten
1/4 cup milk
Butter or margarine

Squeeze grated raw potatoes in a cloth to remove as much moisture as possible. Sift flour with baking powder and salt. Mix grated and mashed potatoes. Add dry ingredients, beaten eggs, and stir together. Add milk to make a batter. Drop by tablespoonfuls onto a hot greased frying pan and cook over moderate heat, allowing about 4 minutes to each side. Serve hot with butter or margarine. *Serves 4.*

Sour Cream Potatoes

These are really good reheated.

6 medium potatoes cooked with skins on, cooled, peeled, and grated
1 1/2 teaspoons salt
1/2 teaspoon pepper
1 pint sour cream
1 bunch green onions, sliced
1 can (4 ounces) diced mild green chilies (optional)
2 cups grated medium-sharp Cheddar cheese

In greased 2-quart flat pan, layer potatoes and sprinkle with salt and pepper. Layer sour cream, onions, green chilies if you want them, and grated Cheddar cheese. Cover and refrigerate overnight. Bake at 350° for 30 to 40 minutes, or until heated through and cheese is melted. *Serves 10.*

Baked Butternut Squash

 1 large butternut squash
 ¼ teaspoon cinnamon
 ¼ teaspoon nutmeg
 ½ cup packed brown sugar
 ½ cup melted butter or margarine
 2 teaspoons lemon juice

Pare squash, remove seeds and fibers, and cut into 1-inch cubes. Place squash in casserole and sprinkle with spices and brown sugar. Drizzle with melted butter or margarine and lemon juice. Bake uncovered in 375° oven for 45 minutes, or until tender. *Serves 8.*

Pattypan Squash

 1 pattypan squash
 Salt and pepper to taste
 3 tablespoons butter or margarine
 3 beaten eggs
 3 tablespoons milk
 Cracker crumbs

Peel squash, remove seeds, and cut in chunks. Simmer in salted water until tender. Mash squash and mix with all ingredients, except cracker crumbs. Place in greased casserole dish and top with cracker crumbs. Dot with more butter or margarine. Bake at 350° for 45 to 60 minutes. *Serves 4.*

FISH AND FOWL

Baked Bass with Mushroom Dressing

1 cup sliced morels or other mushrooms
½ cup butter or margarine
2 cups toasted bread crumbs
Salt and pepper to taste
1 4- to 5-pound bass
Melted butter or margarine

Cook mushrooms in ½ cup butter or margarine until done but still moist. Add bread crumbs and mix well. Salt and pepper cavity of fish. Stuff fish no more than ⅔ full with dressing. Close opening with skewers. Place in greased shallow baking dish. Cut 3 or 4 gashes in sides of fish so it will keep its shape during baking. Brush fish with melted butter or margarine and baste during baking. Bake at 350° for 20 to 30 minutes or more, checking frequently, until fish flakes when tried with fork. *Serves approximately 8.*

Deep-Fried Bass

Fillet bass and cut in 2-inch chunks about 1 inch thick. Heat 1 quart vegetable shortening or salad oil in heavy skillet or deep fryer to 375°. Dip fish in Beer Batter (see below) and drop in hot oil. Fry until golden brown and fish flakes easily. Remove from oil and drain on paper towels. Salt and pepper to taste. *Yield depends on size of the fish. A 5-pound bass serves 7 or 8.*

Beer Batter

1½ cups flour
1½ cups beer

Combine and let set at room temperature for 4 to 5 hours. *Makes about 3 cups.*

Crispy Batter for Fish

1 cup all-purpose flour
2 teaspoons baking powder
1¼ teaspoons salt
2 teaspoons sugar
1 teaspoon salad oil
1 cup water

Mix and sift dry ingredients. Add oil to water. Make a well

in the dry ingredients and slowly pour in liquid, stirring until well blended. *Makes enough for 2 pounds of fish.*

Clam Spaghetti Sauce

1/2 cup chopped onion
3 cloves garlic, minced
1/4 cup olive oil
1 tablespoon fresh minced parsley
1 cup water
1 cup canned tomatoes, chopped
1 can (8 ounces) tomato sauce
1/4 teaspoon oregano
1/4 teaspoon thyme
1 teaspoon salt
1/2 teaspoon pepper
1/2 teaspoon paprika
2 (6 1/2-ounce) cans minced clams
    with juice

Sauté onion and garlic in oil. Add remaining ingredients, except clams with juice, and simmer for 30 minutes. Add clams and juice and reheat. Serve over cooked spaghetti. *Serves 4.*

Crawdads

There is a little lake in northern Washington where crawdads abound. Half the fun is going after them and the rest is having a picnic after they're cooked.

Water
Salt

Crawdads
Melted butter
Lemon juice

Bring a large kettle of salted water to a boil (½ cup salt to 1 gallon water). Put crawdads in boiling water and simmer until they turn deep red. Break off tails. Serve with melted butter flavored slightly with lemon juice. Each person is responsible for shelling his or her own.

Fried Black Crappie

Black crappie are small fish, 3 or 4 to a pound, white-fleshed and very mild in taste. They remind me of overgrown sunfish. They lurk in shallow water under logs or docks and can be caught easily with worms or even a small piece of chamois on a hook.

8 black crappie
8 slices bacon
¼ cup cornmeal
¼ cup flour
½ cup milk
Salt and pepper to taste

Clean and skin crappie. Fry bacon until crisp. Remove bacon and keep warm, reserving grease. Combine cornmeal and flour. Dip fish in milk and then in cornmeal mixture. Fry in the bacon grease until golden brown and fish flakes easily. Salt and pepper to taste. Serve with bacon. *Serves 4.*

SMOKED FISHERMAN

Kokanee, the fresh-water version of the sockeye salmon, is a major preoccupation of fishermen who live in the vicinity of Idaho's Lake Pend Oreille. When I was growing up, the lake's population of kokanee was so dense that it was open to commercial fishing with hand lines. The Troll and her friend Jo Hanson decided this would be a fun way to pick up some extra cash. They fished mostly during January and February, the worst possible months to be on Pend Oreille. The lake is huge and has a well-earned reputation for sudden storms of the lethal variety. Nevertheless, Troll and Jo went out each day in a tiny aluminum boat, often rising and plummeting to the rhythm of mountainous waves, to catch their limit of fish. Coated with ice from freezing spray, by the end of the day their boat looked more like a large, elongated ice cube than a fishing craft. To keep some of the cold at bay, they installed a woodburning heater amidship. It was an amusing sight, these two grimly determined women putting out to fish in a boat loaded down with firewood and belching out more smoke than a Mississippi paddle wheeler. Being an ignorant and naive lad, I once accepted an invitation to accompany them for a day's fishing.

I was assigned a seat in the back of the boat, amid the fuel tanks, with the heater a good nine or ten inches away from my legs. The temperature hovered somewhere around absolute zero, and the Troll stoked up the fire until the heater's tin sides took on a glowing pinkish hue. I tried to get away from the heater, but there was nowhere to go unless I chose to sit atop the outboard motor. The hair on my legs began to curl up and then to smoke, and I might have ignited completely had not the rest of me been coated with a protective layer of ice. "How do you like it so far?" the Troll asked. I told her I was trying to think of a fishing trip on which I'd been more miserable but none came to mind. She was pleased to hear this, and thanked me for sharing it with her. Much as I pleaded, the Troll refused to take me to shore until she and Jo had caught their limit of two hundred kokanee each, and they had already caught three. My one hope was that they would have to go to shore for a rest-room break, at which time I could escape from the boat and make my way to safety through deep snow over a minor range of the Rocky Mountains. "Have some more coffee, ladies," I said. They replied thanks, but no. If they drank any more coffee, they explained, they would have to go to shore for a rest-room break before they had caught their limits. Actually, sitting atop a fifteen-horse outboard motor for six hours isn't as uncomfortable as you might think. Pretty close, though.

Canned Kokanee

Kokanee are our favorite canned fish. When canned with just salt and vinegar, it is difficult to tell them from canned salmon purchased in a store, except they are better.

Clean and scale fish, removing head, tail, and fins. Cut into chunks 2 or 3 inches long. Pack fish tightly in sterilized pint jars to within 1 inch of the top. Add 1/2 teaspoon salt and 1 teaspoon vinegar to each jar. Fish must be canned in a pressure canner. It is necessary to check with your home extension agent to determine length of time and pressure to use for your area.

For a different flavor in the fish, you can add 3 tablespoons French, Russian, or Catalina dressing, or 3 tablespoons catsup to the jars.

Kokanee (Salmon) Quiche

CRUST:

1¼ cups whole wheat flour
¾ cup sharp Cheddar cheese, shredded
⅓ cup walnuts, chopped
½ teaspoon salt
½ teaspoon paprika
7 tablespoons salad oil

Combine all ingredients, except oil. Add oil last and mix thoroughly. Set aside ½ cup crust mixture. Press remaining mixture into bottom and up sides of 10-inch quiche or pie pan. Bake at 400° for 10 minutes.

FILLING:

1 can (15 ounces) salmon or 1 pint kokanee
3 eggs, beaten
1 cup sour cream
⅓ cup mayonnaise
⅔ cup sharp Cheddar cheese, grated
3 tablespoons onion, grated
1 tablespoon dried dill weed
Dash of Tabasco sauce

Drain salmon or kokanee and save enough liquid to make ½ cup. Remove skin and bones from fish, flake, and set aside. Combine eggs, sour cream, mayonnaise, and fish liquid. Stir in remaining ingredients. Spoon into pie crust and sprinkle with reserved crust mixture. Bake at 325° for 1 hour, or until center is firm. *Serves 8.*

Brine for Smoked Kokanee

1 gallon water
1½ cups pickling salt
1 cup brown sugar
1 teaspoon garlic salt
1½ teaspoons white pepper
1 teaspoon allspice
1 teaspoon nutmeg
1 teaspoon marjoram
1 teaspoon thyme

Let cleaned and scaled kokanee soak overnight in brine. The next day dry and smoke fish.

REVENGE OF THE PERCH

*P*erch, in my opinion, are far better eating than any trout. The one problem with perch is that there is no catch or possession limit on them. As a result, anglers sometimes get caught up in a catching frenzy, and by the time they come to their senses they have fifty or sixty perch on their string. Perch have their own method of punishing such greed. First of all, they insist upon being skinned before being fried. Skinning perch is not at all unpleasant, and with a little practice one can become quite skilled at it. Skinning perch can even be fun if, like me, you have a low fun threshold. In order to have fun skinning perch, you must do it early in the day, while you are rested, comfortable, and relaxed. Perch are never skinned under such conditions in real life, however. In case you are wondering, this is why you have skinned thousands of perch over the years and never once thought of it as fun. In real life, perch are skinned only late at night when you are wet, cold, tired, and hungry and have a headache. With a sigh and a moan, you dump your mess of fifty perch out on your cleaning table. They stare up at you gleefully with their dead eyes. "We got you now, sucker!" they say. "We'll teach you to be a fish hog!" You clean and skin the first ten perch. Then you notice that you haven't even put a dent in the catch. You count the unskinned perch. There are still fifty! Frantically, you clean and skin twenty more and recount. Now there are sixty unskinned perch! They are multiplying faster than you can skin and clean them! Midnight comes and goes and you are still at the cleaning table, muttering incoherently to yourself amid great piles of unskinned perch. The perch are laughing at you. You are going mad. This is The Revenge of the Perch, soon to be made into a major movie.

Fried Perch

> 10 perch
> Flour
> Salt and pepper
> Butter or margarine

Clean and skin perch. Roll fish in flour and season to taste with salt and pepper. Heat butter or margarine over medium heat, being sure it doesn't brown. Fry the fish to a golden brown. They are done when the flesh flakes easily. *Serves 5.*

Smoked Salmon or Large Trout

Harvey Felton has probably done other things in life besides fish, but I don't know what they are. He and his wife, Marilyn, live on the shore of Lake Pend Oreille so as never to get too far from the fishing. Harvey's smoked fish are the best I've ever tasted. Here is his recipe.

1 pound pickling salt
1 teaspoon black pepper
1 teaspoon white sugar
1 teaspoon saltpeter

Mix the above ingredients thoroughly. For fish up to 3 pounds, sprinkle mixture in cavity of fish. For fish over 3 pounds, it is best to split the fish and apply mixture to both sides; approximately 1 tablespoon in cavity of smaller fish, 3 tablespoons on each half fish in the 7-to-10-pound range. Place salted fish in container for 72 hours, keeping in a cold place. Remove fish from container and rinse lightly. Hang fish so they can dry for at least 24 hours. When fish have been dried off, they can be placed in a refrigerator for a day or so before smoking. Lay fish in smoker for 4 hours or more, turning fish at least once. Smoker should reach 175° during process. Heat helps remove excess oil. After smoking fish once or twice, you will be able to arrive at the amount of salt and length of smoking time that suit you best.

*E*veryone in the family was astonished when my nephew Mike Gass earned his Ph.D. Up until then, we had regarded Mike as fairly normal. We were even proud of him. He was a helicopter pilot flying combat missions in Vietnam before he turned twenty. After the service, he flew helicopters for the U.S. Forest Service. Then suddenly he went off to school and got himself a Ph.D., the first one ever to show up in our family. It's kind of frightening, when you think of it.

Mike is my steelheading partner. Despite his Ph.D., I let him hang around with me, because he is not only a great steelheader but a fine storyteller. Whether he's tied into a big fish or a tall tale, it's impossible to break his concentration. On a fishing trip one time, we were sleeping in the back of my station wagon, and Mike had just got started on a story, when I suddenly heard the call of nature.

"So Tuck and I had just loaded the drift boat on the trailer . . ." Mike was saying, when I interrupted, or thought I had.

"Just a second, Mike," I said, "I have to step outside for a minute."

I stepped outside into a pitch-dark night, felt my way around the back of the station wagon, and disappeared into empty space. I had forgotten we had parked alongside a twenty-foot drop-off. I picked myself up and tried to climb the bank, but it was too steep. I fought my way through the brush looking for an easier ascent. But a stream blocked my way. There was nothing to do but wade across it, slipping and sliding on the rocks and fighting the current every inch of the way. I finally made it to the far side of the stream, where I ran into brush so thick it was almost impassable. I knew Mike would wonder what had happened to me and start to worry. He was probably outside calling for me right then, but by now I was several hundred yards away and probably couldn't hear him. I finally found a place where I could crawl back up to the road, and did so, but only after sliding back to the bottom of the bank several times. Finally I hiked back to the station wagon and opened the door, expecting Mike to say, "Where in the heck have you been?" But what I heard was: ". . . and then Tuck says to me, 'Why, I thought you snapped the tie-downs closed.' Well, all along I had thought Tuck . . ."

Besides being a great raconteur, Mike is one of the best steelhead cooks I know. Here is one of his recipes.

Baked Steelhead in Cream Sauce

For a smoky flavor, it is ideal to cook this recipe in an open pan on a barbecue.

1 2- to 3-pound steelhead fillet
1 cup heavy cream
6 teaspoons lemon juice
3 tablespoons minced onion
2 teaspoons fresh chopped parsley
Salt and pepper to taste

Remove all bones. Rub your finger across the inside surface to detect the row of bones that extend horizontally into the meat. These can be removed using a pair of pliers. Mix cream, lemon juice, onion, and parsley. Pour over fish. Bake at 425° for about 20 minutes or until fish flakes easily. Salt and pepper to taste. *Serves 4 to 6.*

TROUT, GARNISHED WITH RITUAL

As far as I'm concerned, the rainbow trout is a fish designed by God primarily for catch and release. It is a worthy and gallant adversary for the fly fisherman, but for eating it leaves something to be desired, namely flavor. The humble brook trout is far superior to the rainbow on a dinner plate, and it has also provided me with many fine hours of fishing on Sand Creek. There is, however, a method of cooking rainbow trout that elevates it beyond the mere culinary mode and into a realm approaching ecstasy, the next stop after euphoria.

I should mention first of all that if you are bothered by rituals you probably shouldn't read further, because this method of cooking rainbow trout is definitely a ritual. Ever since we were youngsters, Vern Schulze and I have fished a high mountain stream in Idaho known as X Creek, one of the few streams in the country containing only native rainbows. (Don't bother trying to find X Creek on a map, because you won't.) In the early days, there were no roads into the creek, and we had to hike over the mountains to get to it. At that time, we were probably the only ones to fish X Creek with any regularity, because it was so difficult to get to. The fishing was fantastic in those days, back before logging roads were built into the creek and the unsightly virgin forests eradicated. If your line dropped in the water while you were wading across the creek, a fish would snap up the fly and make a nuisance of itself, tearing off downstream with your line, jumping and thrashing about, until you sighed with exasperation and hauled it in. You couldn't cast a fly without some fish grabbing it. Sometimes the water would boil around the fly, with half a dozen rainbows fighting to get hold of it, and you would become irritated with them and snap the fly away and not let any of them have it, just to teach them a lesson.

When we fished X Creek, Vern and I always carried a sheet of aluminum foil, some salt and pepper, a cube of butter, and some bread. About noon, we built a little driftwood fire on a rocky beach and cleaned a few trout. The trout were placed in the foil with the cube of butter, salted and peppered, and placed on the coals. If we wanted the fish crisp, we left the foil open; if not, we sealed it. From time to time, we added a bit of sand to the fish, but this was not so much a matter of choice as accident. While the fish cooked, we filled our hats with dessert, usually huckleberries but sometimes wild raspberries or blackcaps. (It's a good idea to avoid puddings when you're using your hat for a dessert dish.) When the fish were done we ate them smoking hot out of the foil with our fingers, saying to each other, "Oooch! Ow ow! Boy, are these fish ever—ouch ouch!—good!" I have eaten fish in fine restaurants all over the world, but I have yet to find any that compare with the fresh native rainbow trout cooked in foil on a little rocky beach on X Creek. The secret is in the ritual. For example, a fork must never be used for eating the fish, because that violates the ritual. The fish must always be cooked in foil on a rocky beach on X Creek. Your fishing partner must be Vern. (It is possible, however, to substitute your own version of X Creek and your own Vern.) And you must recite the litany just right. Repeat after me—"Oooch! Ow ow! Boy, are these fish . . ." Sand fish to taste.

Deep-Fried Trout

12 medium-size trout
2 eggs
4 tablespoons water
Flour seasoned with salt, pepper, and a
   touch of onion and garlic powder
Cracker crumbs, finely crushed
Vegetable shortening or salad oil for frying

Clean, scale, and chill trout. Leave whole unless they are over 9 inches in length. Otherwise, split lengthwise. Drain well. Beat eggs with water. Roll trout in seasoned flour, then dip in egg mixture, and roll in cracker crumbs. Heat 3 inches of shortening or oil to 375° and fry fish until golden brown and flesh flakes easily. *Serves 6.*

Fried Trout

½ pound bacon
6 pan-size trout

½ cup cornmeal
Salt and pepper

Fry bacon until crisp, remove from pan, and keep warm. Roll fish in cornmeal and fry in hot bacon grease until crisp and golden brown, turning once. When cooked, they will flake easily with a fork. Salt and pepper to taste. Serve with strips of bacon. *Serves 3 hungry people.*

Trout with French Dressing

6 pan-ready trout
¼ cup French dressing
Salt and pepper
6 thin lemon slices

Preheat oven to 450°. Brush cavity of the trout with French dressing. Sprinkle with salt and pepper. Cut lemon slices in half and put two halves in each cavity. Place fish in greased baking dish and brush tops of fish with remaining French dressing. Bake at 450° for 15 minutes, or until fish flakes easily. *Serves 3.*

Trout Kabobs

2 pounds trout, cut into 1-inch chunks
1 teaspoon celery salt
1 teaspoon onion salt
3 tablespoons brown sugar
Dash of Tabasco sauce

1 cup chili sauce
1/3 cup salad oil
1/4 cup lemon juice

Place chunks of trout in a large bowl. Combine remaining ingredients, pour over trout, and marinate for several hours. Drain and thread on skewers. Broil over coals or in broiler, turning and basting occasionally with marinade, until trout flakes easily, about 10 minutes. *Serves 4 to 5.*

Braised Wild Duck

2 wild ducks
Flour
Vegetable shortening
1 cup white wine
1 bay leaf
1 small onion, chopped
1 teaspoon salt
1 sprig parsley
3 peppercorns
Water

Clean birds and soak in salt water for 3 to 4 hours. Remove and dry well. Cut birds into serving-size pieces and rub with flour. Fry in vegetable shortening until golden brown. Add white wine, bay leaf, chopped onion, salt, parsley, and peppercorns. Cover and simmer until tender. Remove duck pieces to platter and strain juices; thicken slightly with flour and water and correct seasonings. Pour over duck. *Serves 4.*

Roast Wild Duck

1 wild duck
1 cup prunes
1 cup onion, chopped
Flour
Salt and pepper
6 to 8 bacon strips

Soak cleaned and plucked bird overnight in salt water. Dry thoroughly inside and out. Stuff with prunes and chopped onion. Sprinkle with flour, salt, and pepper, and cover breast with bacon strips. Bake at 500° for 15 minutes in uncovered pan for rare. For medium to well-done, bake at 500° for 15 minutes, then reduce heat to 350° and bake for another 15 to 30 minutes, depending on how well-done you like it. Remove prunes and onion and discard after the meat is cooked. *Serves 3.*

Vic's Roast Wild Goose

1 goose
Salt and pepper
Poultry seasoning
Cider vinegar
3 cloves garlic, halved
1 onion, quartered

Clean goose and discard all visible fat. Rub body cavity with salt, pepper, poultry seasoning, and sprinkle with vinegar. Place halved garlic cloves and onion inside cavity. Put on rack in shallow roasting pan and roast at 325° for 20 to 25 minutes per pound. Remove melted grease as it accumulates. *Serves 5.*

Roast Wild Goose with Sauerkraut

The goose will not taste of the kraut; it only makes it moist and improves the flavor.

    1 wild goose
    2 cups sauerkraut
    2 apples, peeled and chopped
    Butter or margarine
    Pepper to taste

Stuff the goose with sauerkraut and apples. Rub butter or margarine and pepper over the outside. Bake at 350° until tender. Serve the stuffing with the goose. *Serves 5.*

Fricasseed Grouse

    4 grouse, cleaned and cut in halves
    Flour
    Salt and pepper
    Butter or margarine
    Rich milk

Roll grouse in flour and sprinkle with salt and pepper. Fry in butter or margarine until well browned. Place in casserole and cover with rich milk. Bake at 350° for an hour or until tender. Remove grouse and thicken milk gravy with flour and water, if necessary. Season to taste and pour over grouse. *Serves 4.*

Tasty Pheasant

    1 pheasant, cut into serving-size pieces
    ³/₄ cup flour
    1 teaspoon salt
    ¹/₄ teaspoon pepper
    ¹/₂ cup salad oil
    1 cup heavy cream
    White cooking wine (optional)

Dredge pheasant in flour seasoned with salt and pepper; brown in hot oil. Arrange in covered casserole; add cream. Bake, covered, at 375° for 2 hours or until tender. Add water as needed. Baste occasionally with cream and drippings. If desired, add a small amount of white wine the last 30 minutes of baking time to tenderize and add flavor. *Serves 3.*

Baked Pheasant with Sauce

This recipe was given to me for chicken. It works equally well on any small game birds.

    1 jar (8 ounces) Catalina dressing
    1 envelope dry onion-soup mix

½ pint apricot jam (apricot-pineapple jam may be substituted)

2 pheasants, cut in pieces

Mix dressing, soup mix, and jam; pour over pheasant pieces. Let marinate 2 or 3 hours. Place in baking pan and pour remaining sauce over top. Bake at 350° for 1 hour, or until tender. *Serves 4.*

Pheasants in Cream

2 2½-to-3-pound pheasants, ready for cooking
Butter or margarine
2 cups tart apples, peeled and chopped
½ cup plus 1 tablespoon applejack
2 cups heavy cream
¼ cup lemon juice
Salt and pepper to taste
1 tablespoon cornstarch

Truss the pheasants and brown them lightly in butter or margarine in a heavy skillet. Remove and keep warm while you sauté the apples in the same skillet. Spread apples in casserole dish and place the pheasants on top. Pour ½ cup applejack in the skillet and stir over heat, scraping the bottom of the pan. Pour over the birds, cover the casserole, and bake in 375° oven for 45 minutes. Add the cream, lemon juice, salt and pepper to taste. Cook uncovered for 30 minutes more, basting occasionally until the birds are tender when pricked with a fork. The drumsticks should move easily. Remove the birds to a hot serving platter. Combine cornstarch with the remaining 1 tablespoon applejack and stir this paste into the liquid in the casserole. Cook the sauce on top of the stove until thick. Strain it over the birds. *Serves 6.*

Roast Pheasant

    1 3-pound pheasant
    Salt and pepper to taste
    1 clove garlic, crushed
    ¼ cup minced celery
    Bacon
    1 large onion, sliced
    2 (4-ounce) cans mushrooms, drained
    1 cup chicken broth

Sprinkle pheasant inside and out with salt and pepper. Place garlic and celery in cavity and tie legs together. Turn wings under. Cover pheasant with bacon strips and place breast side up in roaster. Spread onion slices and mushrooms around bird and pour chicken broth over all. Bake in 350° oven 30 minutes per pound or until tender, basting frequently with pan juices. *Serves 3 to 4.*

Baked Wild Turkey

    2 3-pound wild turkeys, cut in quarters
    6 tablespoons honey
    Salt and pepper to taste
    ½ cup butter or margarine, melted
    1½ cups dry wine
    1 tablespoon chopped fresh parsley

1 medium onion, chopped
1½ cups chicken broth

Brush turkey quarters with honey. Sprinkle with salt and pepper to taste. Bake at 450° for 30 minutes, basting frequently with butter or margarine. Mix remaining ingredients and pour over turkey. Reduce heat to 300°, cover pan, and bake until turkey is tender, approximately 1½ hours. *Serves 6 to 8.*

Mom's Fried Chicken

Mom didn't fry chicken every Sunday, just every other Sunday. There was a great deal of preparation to get ready to fry the chicken. She first gathered her help. The wood box had to be filled to the brim and after the stove was lit, the dampers were juggled around until the heat was perfect. Next, the right cast-iron skillet was selected.

Mom always saved back about ½ cup drippings from the previously fried chicken. To this she added ¼ cup butter or margarine and ¼ cup vegetable shortening. She felt the drippings added a special flavor to the chicken. While this was heating to a moderately high heat, the chicken was rolled in flour. When the skillet reached the correct heat, the chicken was added. Mom salted it in the pan and was very generous when she sprinkled it with black pepper. She said if a little pepper was good for fried chicken, lots of it was better. The chicken was turned frequently and cooked until very crisp and the juices ran clear when pricked to the bone with a fork. *One chicken serves 4.*

Chicken and Dumplings

1 large stewing chicken
2 carrots, chopped
1 onion, chopped
Salt and pepper to taste
Water to cover
1 package frozen peas (optional)
Mrs. Whipple's Dumplings (see p. 63)

Place chicken, carrots, onion, and seasoning in large, heavy Dutch oven or kettle. Add water to cover. Cook over medium heat until the vegetables are done and the chicken is tender. A package of frozen peas can be added just before the chicken is done. Mix dumplings and drop by tablespoons into simmering liquid. Cover with tight lid, and cook over medium heat for 20 minutes. *Serves 4.*

Roast Turkey

Wash and dry turkey. Cover entire turkey with melted vegetable shortening. Place turkey breast side up in shallow roasting pan. Salt, pepper, and sprinkle lightly with poultry seasoning inside and out. Place meat thermometer in thickest part of thigh, being careful not to touch bone. Roast at 325° until thermometer registers 185°. If turkey is getting too brown, cover with a tent of aluminum foil. Remove tent about ¹/₂ hour before turkey is done.

TIMETABLE FOR TURKEY

Weight	Roasting Time at 325°
6–8 pounds	3–3¹/₂ hours
8–12 pounds	3¹/₂–4¹/₂ hours
12–16 pounds	4¹/₂–5¹/₂ hours
16–20 pounds	5¹/₂–6¹/₂ hours
20–24 pounds	6¹/₂–7 hours

Turkey Dressing

Simmer turkey neck in salted water to cover until done. Remove meat from bones, chop, and add to 1 to 2 cups broth:

1¹/₂ cups chopped onion
2 cups chopped celery
1 cup butter or margarine
2 loaves (1 pound) white bread, toasted and cut in cubes
1 cup minced fresh parsley
2 eggs, beaten
Salt and pepper to taste
3 to 4 teaspoons poultry seasoning
1–2 cups turkey broth

Sauté onion and celery in butter or margarine until tender-crisp. Combine remaining ingredients and stir in broth, until desired consistency is reached. Pour into greased, 3-quart casserole dish and bake at 325° for about 1¹/₂ hours. *Serves 15 to 18.*

MEATS

When they were about twelve, my nephew Shaun and one of his friends were hauled up in the mountains by his mother, the Troll, and left to camp for a few days. (Worried by his mother's enthusiastic cooperation in the venture, Shaun dropped white pebbles all along the route, but Troll picked them all up on her way back.) Scarcely had the camping trip begun than it began to pour down rain. After a few days of steady rain, Troll ordered me up into the mountains to retrieve the boys. I found their pup tent pitched in a foot-deep puddle of water, with no signs of life anywhere. I waded into the puddle, opened the flap of the tent, and peered nervously inside. Shaun and his friend were in their sleeping bags, which were almost completely submerged in water. "Well," Shaun said, water lapping about his blue lips, "so much for woodcraft." Since then, we have never allowed Shaun to select a campsite. Otherwise, he is a fine woodsman and excellent camp chef.

Shaun's Bear Roast

    3- to 4-pound leg roast from young bear
    ½ cup cider vinegar
    ½ cup Burgundy wine
    Salt and pepper to taste
    Garlic
    Vegetable shortening

Marinate roast in vinegar-and-wine mixture for several hours. Save liquid. When ready to roast, season meat with salt, pepper, and slivers of garlic placed in small cuts in roast. Brown in shortening. Cover with marinade and cook over low heat until meat is done. Bear meat should be treated the same as pork and be thoroughly cooked. *Serves 8.*

Grilled Elk Chops

    4 elk chops, approximately 1 inch thick
    Salt and pepper to taste
    Garlic powder and onion powder to taste

Season chops to taste with salt, pepper, garlic powder, and onion powder. Grill should be medium hot. Place chops on grill, turning once, and cook to desired doneness. *Serves 4.*

Big Game Steak Kabobs

Great with elk, moose, or deer steak.

1 cup salad oil
1 cup Burgundy wine
1 onion, diced
6 slices bacon, fried and crumbled
Tenderloin or steak, cut into 1-inch cubes
Green peppers, cut in pieces
Canned whole onions, drained

Combine oil, wine, diced onion, and bacon in glass baking dish. Add meat cubes and marinate at room temperature for 4 or 5 hours. Place meat cubes on long skewers, alternating them with vegetables. Cook over hot coals, basting with marinade frequently, until meat reaches desired state of pink. For those who prefer meat well-done, place meat and vegetables on separate skewers. *Two pounds of steak will serve 6.*

Elk or Venison Pasties

You can eat and fish at the same time with these.

CRUST:

3 cups flour
1 teaspoon salt
2/3 cup vegetable shortening
Water

Blend flour, salt, and shortening until mixture resembles corn-meal. Sprinkle on water as you mix with fork until dough can be gathered together. Divide into 6 parts. Roll out into thin round circles.

FILLING:

2 pounds venison or elk steak, cubed
5 potatoes, sliced
1 small onion, chopped
1 large carrot, diced
Salt and pepper to taste
6 tablespoons butter or margarine

Combine venison, potatoes, onion, and carrot; salt and pepper to taste. Divide into 6 parts and place on lower half of each rolled crust. Place 1 tablespoon butter on top of each filling. Fold crust over and seal edges. Prick each pastry 3 or 4 times on top with fork. Bake at 450° for 20 minutes; reduce heat to 375°, and cook for 30 minutes, or until filling is tender and crusts are golden brown. *Serves 6.*

Spicy Elk Pot Roast

½ pound bacon
2 onions, chopped
Flour
Salt and pepper to taste
4-pound elk pot roast
1 tablespoon pickling spice
¼ cup cider vinegar
4 tablespoons brown sugar
1 pint stewed tomatoes

Fry bacon until crisp, remove from pan, and crumble. Sauté onions in bacon grease until golden. Sprinkle flour, salt, and pepper over roast and brown on all sides. Combine remaining ingredients, except for bacon, and pour over roast. Cover and cook slowly on top of stove for approximately 3 hours or until tender, being sure to add water if liquid in the bottom of pan gets too low. When meat is tender, remove from pan and strain juices. Add crumbled bacon, flour, and cold water to juices to make gravy. *Serves 8.*

Barbecued Elk Steak

3 pounds elk round steak
Vegetable shortening
½ cup chopped onion
1 cup catsup
1 cup water
2 tablespoons prepared mustard
2 tablespoons brown sugar
1 teaspoon salt
Pepper to taste
1 teaspoon chili powder
¼ cup cider vinegar
1 tablespoon Worcestershire sauce

Brown steaks in hot shortening on both sides, remove, and put in baking pan. Brown chopped onion slightly, add remaining ingredients, and simmer for 5 minutes. Pour over steaks and cover with lid. Bake in 350° oven for 1 hour or until tender. *Serves 8.*

Baked Elk Steak with Onion

This recipe can be used for any kind of wild meat.

2 pounds elk (or other game) steak
Flour
Vegetable shortening
1 envelope dry onion-soup mix
2 cups beef broth
Water
Salt and pepper to taste

Pound steak, dredge in flour, and cut into serving-size pieces. Brown in hot shortening. Put pieces in casserole and sprinkle with onion-soup mix. Pour beef broth over all, cover, and bake at 325° for 30 to 45 minutes or until tender. Thicken broth with additional flour and water; taste for seasoning. Serve gravy over the meat. *Serves 6.*

Elk Stew with Dumplings

2 pounds elk meat, cut in 1½-inch cubes
Vegetable shortening
1 cup chopped onion
4 cups boiling water
Salt and pepper to taste
1 teaspoon paprika
½ bay leaf
3 large potatoes, peeled and quartered
6 carrots, halved

2 stalks celery, sliced
Mrs. Whipple's Dumplings (see p. 63)

Brown meat in shortening in Dutch oven. Add onion, boiling water, and spices. Cover and simmer for 1½ hours, or until meat is almost tender. Add potatoes and vegetables and simmer until vegetables are partially cooked. Add more boiling water if liquid is low. Drop dumplings into bubbling stew with a tablespoon, cover with lid, and cook on low heat 20 minutes without removing lid. *Serves 6.*

Elk Swiss Steak

Flour
Salt and pepper to taste
2 pounds elk steak
1 large onion, sliced
1 cup sliced mushrooms
Vegetable shortening
2 cloves garlic, minced
1 cup water
1 teaspoon dry mustard
2 tablespoons Worcestershire sauce
2 cups canned tomatoes

Pound flour, salt, and pepper into the elk steak. Sauté onion and mushrooms in shortening until just tender. Remove onion and mushrooms from pan and brown the steak on both sides. Cover with the onion and mushrooms. Mix the rest of the ingredients together and pour over top. Cover and bake in 350° oven for 2 to 2½ hours or until tender. Remove meat from pan and thicken juices with flour and cold water. Pour over steak. *Serves 6.*

Moose Steak

2 pounds moose steak, ½ inch thick
Flour
Salt and pepper to taste
Vegetable shortening
1 cup hot water

Cut steak into serving-size pieces, dredge in flour, and salt and pepper to taste. With a heavy plate or knife, pound the flour into the steak on both sides, being careful not to cut through the steak. Brown on both sides in hot shortening. Add hot water. Cover and simmer for 30 minutes, or until tender. *Serves 6.*

GENERAL INSTRUCTIONS FOR WILD RABBIT

Skin and clean rabbit and wash well in cold water. Soak in salted water overnight. Drain and cover with fresh water. Remove and dry meat.

Fried Wild Rabbit

1 rabbit, dressed and cut in pieces
Flour
Salt and pepper to taste

1 teaspoon paprika
Salad oil, butter, or margarine
1 chicken bouillon cube
½ cup hot water

Stir spices into flour. Dredge meat in flour mixture until well coated. Brown well on all sides in oil, butter, or margarine. Dissolve bouillon cube in hot water and pour over meat. Cover and cook over low heat for 45 minutes or until tender. *Serves 3.*

Wild Rabbit with Gravy

⅓ cup diced bacon or salt pork
1 2½-pound rabbit
1 cup condensed chicken broth
½ cup water
1 cup light cream

Fry bacon or salt pork until pieces are crisp. Remove from pan. Rinse and pat dry fresh, cut-up rabbit. Add to pan. Cook covered on medium heat, 20 to 25 minutes on each side. Rabbit should be brown and tender. Remove meat and keep warm. Add chicken broth and water to pan. Stir. Boil uncovered for 5 minutes. Add light cream and simmer 2 to 3 minutes. Do not boil. Heat rabbit in sauce for 5 minutes. Add bacon or salt pork. *Serves 3 to 4.*

Wild Rabbit Stew

2 rabbits, cut into serving-size pieces
Flour
Salt and pepper to taste
5 slices bacon
Shortening, if needed
1 clove garlic, minced
3½ cups water
3 large potatoes, cut in chunks
3 carrots, sliced
2 onions, sliced
2 stalks celery, sliced
1 teaspoon paprika
1 cup sour cream

Dredge rabbit in flour and season with salt and pepper to taste. Fry the bacon crisp. Remove bacon from pan and crumble. Add shortening to drippings, if needed. Brown the pieces of meat on all sides. Add garlic and water, cover and simmer until almost tender. Add potatoes and vegetables and cook until tender. Correct seasoning and add paprika, crumbled bacon, and sour cream. Reheat, but do not allow to boil. *Serves 6.*

Mom's Venison Breakfast Steak

4 venison steaks, about ½ inch thick
Flour, salt, and pepper
Vegetable shortening
1 cup water

Flour, salt, and pepper each steak, and brown in shortening. Add 1 cup water, cover pan, and let simmer until the meat is tender. Serve with Sourdough Pancakes (see p. 86). *Serves 4.*

Mom's Canned Venison with Gravy

To a pint of canned venison that has been boiled for 10 minutes, add enough water to make the necessary amount of gravy needed. The amount of water added depends upon the number of people eating: the more people, the more water. Sometimes, but not often, 2 pints of meat would be cooked. Thicken with flour and cold water mixed together; season to taste with salt and pepper, and serve over toast or mashed potatoes. *You can serve any number of people with this dish.*

Dried Venison

1 pint pickling salt
¼ cup brown sugar
1 teaspoon saltpeter
20 pounds venison, cut in 5-pound pieces

Combine salt, brown sugar, and saltpeter. Rub over the meat on all sides. Place meat in a crock for 9 days, being sure meat is in contact with the juices at all times. Remove from crock and hang to dry for 2 days in a cool place. Slice the meat as thin as possible and place in smoker heated to at least 175°. Let smoke for 10 hours or more, but check meat every hour after the first 5 hours. Smoke until meat is dry.

Venison Hamburger

1 pound ground venison
¼ pound ground pork
1 small chopped onion (optional)
1 egg

Mix above ingredients and make into 4 or 5 patties. Cook as you would hamburgers. Because venison has so little fat, the pork tends to hold it together and also improves the flavor. *Serves 3 or 4.*

Venison Jerky

3 pounds venison, partially frozen,
    cut with the grain into narrow strips
⅓ cup Worcestershire sauce
⅓ cup soy sauce
1 teaspoon garlic powder
1 teaspoon onion powder
1 teaspoon pepper

Be sure all fat is removed from the venison. Combine all ingredients and marinate meat overnight. Drain meat well. Hang strips in smoker and let smoke for 12 hours or more. If you don't have a smoker, place meat on wire rack in shallow pan and let dry in oven on lowest heat for 18 hours or until completely dry.

Venison Liver

The liver should come from a freshly killed deer. Mix 1 tablespoon salt in 1 quart milk or buttermilk. After the liver has been washed well and dried, pour the milk over it and let it marinate for at least 2 hours. Remove from the milk and dry thoroughly. Cut liver into 1/2-inch-thick slices and roll in flour. Fry several slices of bacon in skillet until crisp, remove from skillet, and keep warm. In the same skillet, brown the liver on both sides over moderate heat. Season with salt and pepper. Serve the liver and bacon together. Venison liver should not be overcooked; it should be brown on the outside and light pink on the inside. *One pound of liver will serve 3.*

Barbecued Venison Ribs

    6 pounds venison ribs
    Vegetable shortening
    1 large onion, chopped
    1/2 cup chopped celery
    1 clove garlic, minced
    1 bottle (28 ounces) catsup
    1 cup water
    1 teaspoon Heinz 57 sauce
    1 tablespoon Worcestershire sauce
    2 teaspoons chili powder
    1/4 cup cider vinegar
    Salt and pepper to taste
    Dash of Tabasco sauce

Cut ribs into three-rib sections and brown well in shortening. Bring remaining ingredients to a boil and cook for 5 minutes. Pour over ribs. Bake at 350° until tender. *Serves 6 to 8.*

Venison Pot Roast

Flour 3- to 4-pound roast and brown in vegetable shortening in heavy skillet with lid. When well browned, season with salt and pepper. Add 2 cups beef stock to the pan, if you have it on hand; if not, add 2 cups water or tomato juice. After 1½ to 2 hours, add halved carrots, small onions, quartered turnips, sliced celery, ½ bay leaf, and ½ cup water if desired for more juice. Simmer gently for 30 minutes, then add potatoes. Continue cooking until meat is tender and vegetables are cooked (about 1 hour). Remove meat and vegetables from pan. Thicken liquid with flour mixed with cold water to make gravy. Season to taste with salt and pepper. Serve the gravy separately. *Serves 6 to 8.*

Roast Leg of Venison

  1 8-pound venison leg roast
  3 tablespoons salt
  ¼ cup coarsely ground pepper
  5 tablespoons flour
  15 cloves garlic, peeled

Heat oven to 500°. Rub salt and pepper into meat; pat flour over it. Put in large roasting pan and place garlic cloves over and around the meat. Roast for 45 minutes at 500°, then reduce heat to 325° and continue roasting for 1 hour, or more for well-done. Slice thin. *Serves 10.*

Roast Venison

Marinate 4- to 5-pound roast in buttermilk overnight. This eliminates much of the wild flavor. Dry the roast well. Thread bacon strips into larding needle and draw through the meat, about an inch apart. Hold close to the meat by tying with clean string. Sprinkle meat with salt and pepper, and sparingly with garlic powder and onion powder. Place meat in roasting pan without lid. Bake 20 minutes per pound at 325° for rare and 25 to 30 minutes per pound for medium to well-done. When meat is tender, remove from pan to warm platter. To make gravy, pour 1½ cups water into drippings in pan and stir, scraping bottom of pan. Heat to boiling. Thicken with flour and cold-water mixture. Season to taste with salt and pepper. *Serves 6 to 8.*

Beef or Venison Salami

5 pounds ground beef or ground venison
5 teaspoons Morton Tender Quick Salt or
   Morton Complete Cure With Sugar
2½ teaspoons mustard seed
1 teaspoon pepper
2½ teaspoons garlic salt
1 teaspoon hickory-smoked salt

Mix all ingredients well. Put in refrigerator 3 days and knead every day. Make 4 or 5 rolls. Bake at 160° for 8 hours. Cool and keep refrigerated. *Makes 4 to 5 rolls.*

Harvey Felten's Homemade Sausage

Use deer, antelope, elk, or other game.

20 pounds meat and fat trimmings
1 cup salt
⅓ cup black pepper

Other seasoning can be added, such as sage, cayenne pepper, or garlic powder. Always keep in mind that garlic powder and cayenne pepper are potent; a small amount will go a long way. When using venison, remove all tallow from the meat. When using elk or antelope, you can leave a small amount of fat on the meat, but it's better to use pork fat. A good mixture for sausage is a ratio of ⅓ or ¼ pork trimmings (fat) to meat. For example, 20 pounds of game meat needs approximately 5 to 7 pounds pork trimmings.

Cut meat and pork trimmings into small slices. Spread out and sprinkle seasoning on meat, then grind. This gives a nicer-looking sausage than mixing seasoning in sausage after grinding. Only one grinding is necessary. If you have a sausage stuffer, you can buy casings from the local meat market. This makes it possible to smoke the sausage. Twist sausage in casings every 12 inches or so, then hang in smoker for about 2 hours of cold smoking. Otherwise sausage can be used as bulk sausage. *Makes 18 to 19 pounds of smoked sausage; 20 pounds of bulk sausage.*

Breaded Venison Steak

 2 pounds venison steak, thickly cut
 2 eggs, beaten
 4 tablespoons lemon juice
 4 tablespoons water
 2 cups finely crushed soda cracker crumbs
 Vegetable shortening
 Salt and pepper to taste

Cut the venison steak into serving-size pieces. Place steak, a piece at a time, between two pieces of waxed paper and pound with a mallet to approximately 1/3-inch thickness. Blend beaten eggs, lemon juice, and water. Dip each piece of meat in egg mixture and then in cracker crumbs. Place in flat pan with waxed paper between layers. Refrigerate for 5 to 6 hours to firm up meat. Heat shortening in heavy skillet to a medium temperature. Add steaks, salt and pepper to taste, and cook to a golden brown, turning once. *Serves 4.*

Company's Coming Venison Steak

 Butter, margarine, or vegetable shortening
 6 venison steaks, 1 1/2 inches thick
 Salt and pepper to taste
 1 tablespoon lemon juice
 Pinch of cayenne pepper
 1 cup homemade wine or any dry white wine

Heat butter, margarine, or vegetable shortening; add steaks and cook over medium heat, browning well on both sides.

Salt and pepper to taste. Add lemon juice and cayenne pepper to wine and pour over steaks. Simmer uncovered for 10 minutes or until tender. *Serves 6.*

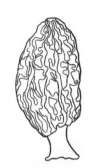

Venison Steak with Morel Mushroom Sauce

Other mushrooms can be substituted, but morels add a special flavor.

Vegetable shortening, butter, or margarine
6 venison steaks, ³/₄ inch thick, pounded until
   ¹/₃ inch thick
Flour
3 tablespoons butter or margarine
1 cup mushrooms, preferably freshly picked morels
1¹/₂ tablespoons flour
1 cup light cream
Salt and pepper to taste

Melt shortening, butter, or margarine in a heavy skillet over moderate heat. Roll steaks in flour and brown on both sides. Remove from pan and keep warm. Melt butter or margarine in the same pan and add the morels. Cook on low heat, stirring frequently, until done, but still moist. Add 1¹/₂ tablespoons flour to mushrooms and stir well. Add light cream and cook, stirring until sauce is slightly thickened. Salt and pepper to taste. Serve the sauce with venison steak. *Serves 6.*

Venison or Beef Stroganoff

2 pounds venison or beefsteak
Flour
Salt and pepper to taste
Vegetable shortening
Butter or margarine
1 cup chopped onions
1/4 pound morels or other mushrooms, sliced
1 clove garlic, minced
3 tablespoons flour
1 1/2 cups beef stock
1/4 cup dry wine
1 cup sour cream
1 teaspoon dried dill weed
Aunt Verda's Noodles (see p. 67)

Slice venison steak into thin strips, coat with flour, and season with salt and pepper. Heat shortening and brown the strips of meat. Remove meat and set aside. In same skillet, melt butter or margarine and sauté onions, mushrooms, and garlic. Sprinkle 3 tablespoons flour on the mixture and stir well. Gradually pour in beef stock, stirring until smooth. Bring to a boil, turn heat to low, and simmer 5 minutes, stirring constantly. Add wine, sour cream, and dill weed. Salt and pepper to taste. If preferred, serve sour cream on the side instead of putting it in the sauce. Be careful not to let mixture boil. Add venison strips and heat through. Serve over hot buttered noodles. *Serves 8.*

Boiled Beef

Use about 3 pounds brisket of beef. Put meat in heavy pot and just barely cover it with boiling water. Bring it back to a boil and turn down the heat. As meat simmers, spoon off grease and scum that rise to the top. After 45 minutes, add a few whole peeled onions, a whole peeled carrot or two, a bay leaf, a celery stalk with leaves, salt and pepper to taste, a few crushed peppercorns, and ½ teaspoon thyme. Cover pot and simmer 3 to 4 hours, or until meat is tender. Save juices in pot for gravies and soups. Slice meat thin and serve with freshly grated horseradish. *Serves 8.*

Beef Pot Roast

    1 4- to 5-pound beef blade pot roast
    Flour
    Salt and pepper to taste
    3 tablespoons vegetable shortening
    1 can (1 pound) whole tomatoes
    2 teaspoons Worcestershire sauce
    1 teaspoon basil
    2 medium-size onions, peeled and cut in quarters
    4 carrots, halved
    2 medium-size zucchini, cut in 1-inch chunks

Dredge meat in flour; sprinkle with salt and pepper on both sides. Brown in shortening. Drain tomatoes, saving juice. Combine juice, Worcestershire sauce, and basil. Add to meat. Add onions and carrots. Cover and bake at 325° for 2½ hours, or until tender. Add zucchini and cook for 15 minutes. Add reserved tomatoes and cook for another 5 minutes, or until heated. Combine flour and water and thicken drippings to make gravy. *Serves 8.*

Roast Beef

Place the rib, rump, or rolled roast fat side up in a roasting pan; sprinkle with salt and pepper to taste. Roast uncovered in 300° oven. Don't open the oven until the meat is done. Rare meat should be roasted 18 to 20 minutes per pound, medium should be roasted 25 minutes per pound, and well-done should be roasted 30 minutes per pound.

German Sausage

15 pounds ground pork shoulder
4 tablespoons salt
3 tablespoons pepper
1 teaspoon sugar
1 teaspoon sage
7 large garlic cloves, minced
1/4 teaspoon allspice

Knead the seasonings into the meat, being sure the meat is kept cold all of the time. Place the mixture in the refrigerator overnight to blend flavors. The next morning put meat in casings, if you wish. If you have more than you can use in a short while, it can be frozen. If you haven't put meat in casings, make patties and fry as you would any sausage. If in casings, simmer in water until cooked. *Makes 15 pounds.*

Vic's Tourtière

Our stepfather, Vic DeMers, was a Frenchman who believed in following his family's holiday traditions, one of which was making pork pies for New Year's Day. He would make ten or twelve pies two or three days before New Year's, wrap them in paper, and place the unbaked pies in stacks out in our back entryway to freeze. Our first introduction to a freezer.

1 pound lean pork, minced
1 small onion, diced
1 clove garlic
³/₄ teaspoon salt
¹/₂ teaspoon sage
2 tablespoons minced celery
¹/₄ teaspoon cloves
¹/₂ cup water
Pie pastry for top and bottom crusts (see p. 227)

Brown pork in skillet and drain off all fat. Combine with rest of ingredients (except pastry) in heavy pan and bring to boil. Reduce heat and cook uncovered for 20 minutes, or until liquid is reduced. The mixture should be damp but not watery. Remove garlic clove. Cool mixture and pour into unbaked pie shell. Cover with top crust and prick top to let steam escape. Bake at 450° for 10 minutes, reduce heat to 350°, and bake until crust is golden brown. *Serves 6.*

CAKES, COOKIES, AND CANDIES

JUST DESSERTS

On my mother's birthday, when she was teaching at the Spirit Lake school, the Troll feigned illness in order to stay home and cook Mom a Lady Baltimore birthday cake. The only problem was that the Troll didn't know how to bake a Lady Baltimore cake, or any other kind of cake either. I was about four and Mom had hired some wretched girl to look after me during the day. Troll asked the girl to bake the cake. The girl said she would be happy to—for a dollar. My sister didn't have a dollar. I was the only one who had a dollar, locked up in a little tin log-cabin bank.

"We'll use your dollar," Troll said.

"No way," I said. "It's locked in the bank and there's no way to get it out, and I don't want it out anyway."

"You selfish little wart," Troll replied. "If we don't use your dollar, Mom won't get a birthday cake."

"Tough!" I said.

Troll then snatched up the bank and, holding me against the wall with a foot planted on my chest, pried the roof off the log cabin with a screwdriver. She paid the money to the wretched hired girl, who then baked the cake. But as the girl was carrying the finished cake out of the kitchen, she tripped and dumped the cake on the floor. In my opinion, the smashed cake had fallen not only onto the floor but into the category of just desserts. The Troll was demolished. After all my sister's scheming and conniving and bank robbery, Mom still had no birthday cake.

Mom arrived home shortly after the mess had been cleaned up and the remains of the cake dumped in the garbage. She was carrying a whole armload of candies and cookies and cupcakes her students had brought her for her birthday. There were still two full-size birthday cakes complete with candles out in the car. It looked like a pretty good haul to me.

"I don't know how the children even knew it was my birthday," Mom said. "It's hard to imagine a bunch of rowdy kids being so thoughtful. I hadn't even expected a birthday cake, let alone all this."

Troll looked pretty glum, but I doubt it was because she was worrying about how to pay me back my dollar. Come to think of it, she never has paid me back that dollar. I'll have to call it to her attention, now that she's too old to plant a foot on my chest.

Aunt Gladys's Lady Baltimore Cake

1 cup vegetable shortening
¹/₂ cup butter or margarine
2 cups sugar
3 cups sifted flour

4 teaspoons baking powder
1 teaspoon salt
1/2 cup milk
1/2 cup water
2 teaspoons vanilla
6 egg whites

Cream the shortening, butter or margarine, and sugar together until fluffy. Sift flour, baking powder, and salt together. Add flour mixture to sugar mixture alternately with milk and water. Stir in vanilla. Beat egg whites stiff and fold into cake mixture. Pour batter into three greased and floured 9-inch cake pans. Bake at 350° for approximately 25 minutes or until cake tests done. Layer with Fruit-Nut Filling, below. Spread with Fluffy White Frosting, p. 192. *Serves 12.*

Fruit-Nut Filling

1 cup sugar
1/2 cup water
Pinch of cream of tartar
2 egg whites
1 cup seedless raisins, cut fine
1 cup chopped walnuts
1 teaspoon vanilla

Cook sugar, water, and cream of tartar together until it threads. Pour gradually into stiffly beaten egg whites. Beat until thick enough to hold a point. Add raisins, walnuts, and vanilla.

Apple Cake

2 cups sugar
4 cups apples, peeled and chopped

½ cup salad oil
1 cup chopped nuts
2 eggs, beaten
2 teaspoons vanilla
2 cups flour
2 teaspoons baking soda
2 teaspoons cinnamon
1 teaspoon salt

Mix sugar through the apples. Combine oil, nuts, eggs, and vanilla, and add to apple mixture. Stir together the flour, baking soda, cinnamon, and salt and add to above mixture, stirring until all ingredients are well mixed. Pour into greased and floured pan (9 × 13 inches). Bake in 350° oven for 60 minutes. This is a moist cake that keeps well. It is especially good served with whipped cream on top. *Serves 15.*

Bourbon Nut Cake

This was our substitute for fruitcake.

½ pound butter
2 cups sugar
6 eggs
4 cups flour, unsifted
1 teaspoon baking powder
1 cup bourbon
1 pound walnuts, chopped
1 pound seedless raisins

Preheat oven to 250°. Cream butter and sugar; add eggs, one at a time, beating in well. Reserve 1 cup flour; sift remaining flour together with baking powder and stir into egg mixture.

Add bourbon and stir in well. Toss reserved 1 cup flour with walnuts and raisins and fold in carefully. Pour mixture into two greased and floured pans (9 × 5 × 3 inches). Bake at 250° for 1½ to 2 hours. Use toothpick test to check that cake is done. Loaves will not be brown. Remove from oven; cool. Keep in refrigerator in bourbon-soaked cheesecloth for as long as cake lasts. *Serves 18.*

Carrot Pineapple Cake

4 eggs
2 cups sugar
1¼ cups salad oil
2 cups flour
2 teaspoons baking powder
1 teaspoon baking soda
½ teaspoon salt
1 teaspoon cinnamon
½ teaspoon nutmeg
½ teaspoon allspice
2 cups grated raw carrots
1 can (8½ ounces) crushed pineapple,
   lightly drained
1 cup chopped walnuts
½ cup flaked coconut

Prepare carrots, pineapple, and walnuts. Grease and flour pan (13 × 9 × 2 inches). Beat eggs lightly, and beat in sugar. Stir in oil, the next seven ingredients, carrots, and pineapple. Mix well. Stir in walnuts and coconut. Spread evenly in pan and bake at 350° for 45 to 60 minutes. When cool, frost with Cream Cheese Frosting, p. 191. *Serves 15.*

Chocolate Picnic Cake

1¼ cups boiling water
1 cup uncooked oatmeal
1 package (6 ounces) chocolate chips (1 cup)
⅓ cup vegetable shortening
½ cup sugar
½ cup packed brown sugar
2 eggs
1½ cups sifted flour
1 teaspoon baking soda
½ teaspoon salt

Pour water over oatmeal; let stand 20 minutes in covered pan. Melt chocolate chips in the top of a double boiler. Remove from heat and cool. Combine all ingredients and beat well. Pour into greased and floured pan (9 × 9 inches). Bake at 350° for 45 to 50 minutes. Remove from oven and, while still warm, spread with Chocolate Cake Frosting, p. 191. *Serves 8.*

Chocolate-Sauerkraut Cake

⅔ cup butter or margarine
1½ cups sugar
3 eggs
1 teaspoon vanilla
2¼ cups flour
½ cup cocoa
1 teaspoon baking powder
1 teaspoon baking soda
1 teaspoon salt
1 cup water
⅔ cup sauerkraut, rinsed, drained, and finely chopped

Cream butter or margarine, sugar, eggs, and vanilla. Sift together the flour, cocoa, baking powder, baking soda, and salt, and add to sugar and egg mixture. Add water and sauerkraut; stir well. Pour into greased and floured pan (9 × 13 inches). Bake at 350° for 35 to 40 minutes. *Serves 15.*

Crazy Cake

1½ cups flour
1 cup sugar
1 teaspoon baking soda
½ teaspoon salt
3 slightly rounded tablespoons cocoa
6 tablespoons salad oil
1 tablespoon cider vinegar
1 teaspoon vanilla
1 cup cold water

Sift together into a glass pan (9 × 9 inches) the flour, sugar, baking soda, salt, and cocoa. Add remaining ingredients, mix thoroughly with fork, and bake at 350° for 30 minutes. *Serves 8.*

Oatmeal Cake

1 cup quick oats
1¼ cups boiling water
1 cup butter or margarine
1 cup white sugar
1 cup packed brown sugar
2 eggs
1½ cups flour

1 teaspoon baking soda
$\frac{1}{2}$ teaspoon salt
$\frac{1}{2}$ teaspoon nutmeg
1 teaspoon cinnamon

Cook oats in boiling water for 1 minute; add butter or margarine. Cover and cool. Beat sugars and eggs together; add cooked oats. Sift together flour, baking soda, salt, nutmeg, and cinnamon. Add to beaten mixture and mix well. Pour into greased and floured pan (9 × 13 inches) and bake at 350° for 30 minutes. Remove cake from oven and spread with topping. *Serves 15.*

TOPPING:

6 tablespoons butter or margarine, melted
$1\frac{1}{2}$ cups packed brown sugar
$\frac{1}{4}$ cup milk
1 cup chopped walnuts
1 cup coconut

Combine all ingredients. Spread on cake and bake another 15 minutes.

Pineapple Upside-Down Cake

$\frac{1}{3}$ cup butter or margarine
$\frac{1}{2}$ cup packed brown sugar
1 can (No. 2) sliced pineapple, drained
$1\frac{1}{2}$ cups flour
$1\frac{1}{2}$ cups sugar
2 teaspoons baking powder
$\frac{1}{2}$ teaspoon salt

⅓ cup soft vegetable shortening
⅔ cup milk
2 teaspoons vanilla
1 egg
1 pint whipping cream

Melt butter or margarine in heavy 10-inch skillet or square pan. Sprinkle brown sugar evenly over butter. Arrange pineapple in pattern over brown sugar. Sift flour, 1 cup of sugar, baking powder, and salt together; add shortening, milk, and 1 teaspoon vanilla. Beat 2 minutes. Add egg; beat 2 more minutes. Pour over pineapple. Bake at 350° for 40 to 50 minutes. Turn cake upside down on serving plate and let cool. Whip cream with ½ cup sugar and 1 teaspoon vanilla for the top of the cake. *Serves 12.*

Pumpkin Roll Cake

3 eggs
1 cup sugar
⅔ cup cooked pumpkin
1 teaspoon vanilla
1 teaspoon lemon juice
¾ cup flour
1 teaspoon baking powder
2 teaspoons cinnamon
1 teaspoon ginger
½ teaspoon salt
½ teaspoon nutmeg
1 cup chopped walnuts
Powdered sugar

Beat eggs, sugar, pumpkin, vanilla, and lemon juice in mixer for 5 minutes. In separate bowl, sift next six ingredients. Fold in pumpkin mixture. Pour into greased and floured jelly-roll pan and sprinkle with walnuts. Bake at 375° for 15 minutes. Turn out on smooth towel sprinkled with powdered sugar and roll up as for jelly roll. Let set to cool. Unroll to fill. *Serves 12.*

FILLING FOR PUMPKIN ROLL CAKE:

2 (3-ounce) packages cream cheese
1 cup powdered sugar
4 tablespoons butter or margarine
1 teaspoon vanilla
1 tablespoon grated orange rind

Combine ingredients and beat until fluffy. Spread filling on cooled cake and reroll. Cut in slices to serve.

Rhubarb Crumb Cake

½ cup white sugar
¼ cup butter or margarine
½ cup flour
½ cup vegetable shortening
1½ cups packed brown sugar
1 egg
1 teaspoon baking soda
1 cup sour cream
2 cups sifted flour
2 teaspoons cinnamon
1½ cups rhubarb, sliced fine
1 teaspoon vanilla
½ cup chopped walnuts

Mix white sugar, butter or margarine, and flour until crumbly. Set aside. Cream shortening, brown sugar, and egg. Mix baking soda and sour cream, and add alternately with the flour and cinnamon to egg mixture. Stir in rhubarb, vanilla, and walnuts. Pour into greased and floured pan (9 × 13 inches) and sprinkle with first mixture. Bake at 350° for 35 to 40 minutes. *Serves 15.*

Mom's Wild Strawberry Shortcake

TOPPING:

6 cups wild strawberries, hulled and rinsed
1 cup sugar
1 pint whipping cream
4 tablespoons sugar
1 teaspoon vanilla

First, plan on several hours for picking wild strawberries. After hulling and rinsing berries, mix gently with 1 cup sugar. Let set until biscuits are through baking.

BISCUIT DOUGH:

2 cups sifted flour
3 teaspoons baking powder
1 teaspoon salt
1 tablespoon sugar
4 tablespoons butter or margarine
¾ cup milk

Sift dry ingredients together. Rub in butter or margarine with fingertips until the consistency of cornmeal. Add milk and mix with fork to a soft dough. Pat out on floured board to ¾-inch thickness. Cut out rounds with biscuit cutter. Place on greased cookie sheet and bake at 450° for 10 to 12 minutes until golden brown.

Whip cream and flavor with 4 tablespoons sugar, or more if you prefer sweeter whipped cream, and 1 teaspoon vanilla. Split the biscuits and lightly butter both sides. Spread lower half of biscuit with strawberries, place top half on berries, and spoon more berries over all. Top with whipped cream. *Serves 6.*

Cream Cheese Frosting

2 (3-ounce) packages cream cheese
1 pound powdered sugar
Dash of salt
2 tablespoons light cream
2 teaspoons vanilla

Beat cream cheese until soft and light. Gradually beat in powdered sugar and salt. Add cream, 1 tablespoon at a time, until mixture reaches spreading consistency. Add vanilla and beat well. *Enough frosting to frost 1 3-layer cake or 1 large sheet cake.*

Chocolate Cake Frosting

¼ cup butter or margarine, melted
½ cup packed brown sugar

3 tablespoons light cream
1/2 cup chopped walnuts
3/4 cup shredded coconut

Combine ingredients. Spread over warm cake and broil until frosting becomes bubbly. *Enough frosting for one 11 × 13 cake.*

Fluffy White Frosting

1 cup plus 2 tablespoons sugar
1/4 cup cold water
3 egg whites
1/4 teaspoon cream of tartar
1 teaspoon vanilla
1/2 teaspoon almond flavoring

Put sugar and water in pan and let set until the sugar is dissolved. Cook over medium to low heat until the syrup spins a thread when dripped from a spoon. Beat egg whites and cream of tartar until stiff, but not dry. When the syrup is ready, pour slowly into the egg whites, beating mixture continually. Beat until the frosting will stand in peaks when beater is raised. Stir in vanilla and almond flavoring. *Will frost a 3-layer cake.*

Dream Bars

1/2 cup butter or margarine
1/2 cup white sugar
1 cup plus 2 tablespoons flour

1 cup packed brown sugar
2 eggs
1 teaspoon vanilla
1/2 cup shredded coconut
1 cup coarsely chopped walnuts
1 cup chopped dates

Mix well the butter or margarine, white sugar, and 1 cup flour. Pat into a shallow pan (9 × 13 inches). Bake at 375° for 10 minutes.

Mix remaining ingredients and spoon over baked part. Bake for 20 minutes more at 375°. Cut in squares when cool. *Makes 48 bars.*

Sugar Plum Bars

Cousin Dorothy has used this recipe for thirty years. The bars keep for a long time. If you don't have mincemeat, use applesauce and seedless raisins, and add a little more allspice and cinnamon.

2/3 cup vegetable shortening
1/2 cup sugar
1 teaspoon grated orange rind
1/2 cup light cream
1/2 cup orange juice
2 cups flour
1/2 teaspoon baking soda
1/2 teaspoon salt
1/2 teaspoon cinnamon
1/2 teaspoon allspice
1/2 cup mixed candied fruit
1/2 cup mincemeat
1/2 cup chopped walnuts

Cream shortening and sugar; add orange rind. Combine cream and orange juice, and add alternately with sifted dry ingredients to creamed sugar and shortening. Fold in fruit, mincemeat, and nuts. Pour into two greased 8-inch-square pans or one greased pan (9 × 13 inches). Bake at 350° for 25 minutes. Cool and frost with Powdered Sugar Icing (see p. 90) that has grated orange rind added to it, and sprinkle with chopped nuts. Cut into squares. *Makes 48 bars*.

Butterballs

1½ cups butter or margarine
1 teaspoon vanilla
1 cup packed brown sugar
2¾ cups flour
White sugar
Walnuts, almonds, or pecans, whole

Combine butter or margarine, vanilla, brown sugar, and flour. Chill dough; form into small balls. Roll in white sugar and press one nutmeat on top of each ball. Bake on ungreased cookie sheet at 375° for 10 minutes. *Makes about 45 cookies*.

Hard-Time Cookies

1 cup sugar
¾ cup bacon grease
1 egg

4 tablespoons light corn syrup
1 teaspoon vanilla
2 cups flour
1 teaspoon baking powder
1 teaspoon baking soda
$1/2$ teaspoon salt
Sugar for rolling

Combine ingredients and mix well. Roll into balls about the size of walnuts, then roll in sugar. Place far apart on greased cookie sheet. Bake at 325° for 10 to 12 minutes. *Makes about 36 cookies.*

Mom's Soft Molasses Cookies

1 cup sugar
$3/4$ cup butter or margarine
2 eggs, well beaten
2 teaspoons baking soda
1 cup molasses
5 cups flour
1 teaspoon ginger
1 teaspoon cinnamon
$1/2$ teaspoon salt
$1/2$ cup sour cream
Sugar for cookie tops

Cream 1 cup sugar and butter or margarine thoroughly and add beaten eggs. Combine baking soda and molasses; add to first mixture. Sift dry ingredients and add alternately with sour cream. Form into balls the size of a walnut, place on greased cookie sheet, and flatten with the bottom of a glass dipped in sugar. Bake at 375° for 15 minutes. *Makes 48 cookies.*

Macaroons

    3 egg whites
    1 cup sugar
    ½ teaspoon vanilla
    ½ cup walnuts
    2 cups cornflakes
    ½ cup shredded coconut

Beat egg whites until stiff. Beat in sugar gradually. Add vanilla. Fold in walnuts, cornflakes, and coconut. Drop by teaspoonfuls onto well-greased cookie sheet. Bake at 350° for 10 to 12 minutes. *Makes approximately 30 cookies.*

Mexican Wedding Cakes

    1 cup butter or margarine
    6 tablespoons powdered sugar
    1 teaspoon vanilla
    2 cups cake flour
    1 cup chopped pecans
    Powdered sugar for rolling

Cream butter or margarine and 6 tablespoons powdered sugar together; add vanilla. Mix in flour and pecans. Roll into small balls; place on ungreased cookie sheet. Bake until golden in 350° oven. Roll in powdered sugar. *Makes about 36.*

Oatmeal Cookies

$^3/_4$ cup butter or margarine
$^3/_4$ cup white sugar
$^3/_4$ cup packed brown sugar
2 eggs
$1^1/_2$ teaspoons vanilla
1 cup flour
$^1/_2$ teaspoon baking soda
$^1/_2$ teaspoon baking powder
$^1/_2$ teaspoon salt
$2^1/_4$ cups quick oatmeal
$^3/_4$ cup finely chopped nuts

Cream butter or margarine, sugars, eggs, and vanilla together. Combine dry ingredients and add gradually to first mixture. Stir in nuts. Drop by tablespoon 3 inches apart on a greased cookie sheet. Bake at 350° for approximately 9 minutes. Remove from pan and place on rack to cool. *Makes about 48 cookies.*

Snickerdoodles

$^1/_2$ cup butter or margarine, softened
$^1/_2$ cup vegetable shortening
$1^1/_2$ cups sugar
2 eggs
$2^3/_4$ cups flour
2 teaspoons cream of tartar
1 teaspoon baking soda
$^1/_4$ teaspoon salt
2 tablespoons sugar
2 teaspoons cinnamon

Cream butter or margarine, shortening, 1½ cups sugar, and eggs. Blend in flour, cream of tartar, baking soda, and salt. Roll teaspoonfuls of dough into balls. Mix remaining sugar and cinnamon, and roll the cookie balls in the mixture. Place 2 inches apart on ungreased cookie sheet and bake at 400° for 8 to 10 minutes. *Makes 72 cookies.*

Applesauce Candy

    2½ cups applesauce
    4 envelopes unflavored gelatin
    4 cups sugar
    1 teaspoon vanilla
    1 cup chopped walnuts
    Powdered sugar

Mix 1 cup applesauce with gelatin to soften. Add 1½ cups applesauce to sugar. Combine both mixtures and simmer over low heat for 15 minutes. Remove from heat; add vanilla and walnuts. Pour into buttered pan (9 × 9 inches) and let cool. When firm, cut into squares and roll in powdered sugar. *Makes 48 pieces.*

All-Weather Divinity

You will need a candy thermometer for this recipe and many of the other candy recipes.

    2⅓ cups white sugar
    ⅔ cup light corn syrup

$^1/_2$ cup water
Dash of salt
2 egg whites at room temperature
$^1/_4$ teaspoon cream of tartar
$^3/_4$ cup walnuts or pecans
1 teaspoon vanilla
$^1/_2$ teaspoon almond flavoring

Combine sugar, syrup, water, and salt. Cook on low heat without stirring until it registers 260° on candy thermometer. It is most important to take the temperature up to 260° and remove from heat promptly. (You need a candy thermometer for divinity—at least I do!) Meanwhile, beat egg whites and cream of tartar until stiff, using electric mixer. Continue beating egg whites while slowly pouring syrup over them. Be sure to pour the syrup in a very small stream. Continue to beat until mixture is no longer shiny and retains its shape when dropped from a spoon. Add nuts and flavorings. Drop by teaspoonfuls onto waxed paper. *Makes about 60 pieces.*

Chocolate Fudge

3 cups sugar
Dash of salt
3 1-ounce squares unsweetened chocolate
1 cup evaporated milk
2 tablespoons light corn syrup
3 tablespoons butter or margarine
2 teaspoons vanilla
1 cup coarsely chopped walnuts

Butter cooking pan (9 × 9 inches) before starting. Combine sugar, salt, chocolate, evaporated milk, and corn syrup. Cook over low heat, stirring until ingredients are well blended. Continue cooking until mixture reaches 234° on candy thermometer, or soft-ball stage. Remove from heat; add butter or margarine and let cool until outside of pan feels lukewarm. Add vanilla and beat candy until creamy and no longer shiny. Stir in walnuts and pour into buttered platter. When firm, cut into squares. *Makes about 50 pieces.*

Golden Fudge

6 cups sugar
½ pound butter or margarine
2 cups dark corn syrup
1 can (14½ ounces) evaporated milk
3 cups walnuts, coarsely chopped
1 teaspoon vanilla

Butter cooking pan (11 × 13 inches) before starting. Cook sugar, butter or margarine, syrup, and evaporated milk over low heat for 30 minutes, stirring frequently. Add nuts; cook over high heat until mixture will form soft ball in cold water or reaches 240° on candy thermometer. Stir constantly. Add vanilla and cool to lukewarm. Beat by hand until fudge loses its gloss and starts to hold its shape. Pour into greased platter. Let set until firm and cut into squares. *Makes about 100 pieces.*

Wedding Mints

1 package (8 ounces) cream cheese
6¾ cups powdered sugar
½ to 1 teaspoon flavoring (see below)
Food coloring

Soften cream cheese at room temperature. Blend in powdered sugar. Divide into 3 parts, flavoring and coloring each part. For peppermint flavoring, use pink coloring; lemon flavoring, use yellow coloring; wintergreen, leave uncolored. Roll mixture into small balls and flatten with a fork. Keep refrigerated. *Makes about 200 mints.*

Peanut Brittle

2 cups white sugar
⅔ cup light corn syrup
½ cup water
1 pound cocktail peanuts
1 teaspoon baking soda

Combine sugar, syrup, and water in large, heavy pan. Place on medium heat and cook to 290°, or hard-crack stage. Add peanuts and cook 10 minutes longer. Stir frequently; increase heat during last 2 minutes to give golden color. Just before removing from heat, add baking soda and mix well; it will bubble. Spread in buttered, shallow-rimmed pan. Cool rapidly and break up when cooled. *Makes about 2 pounds.*

Penuche

1 cup white sugar
2 cups packed brown sugar
1/4 cup light corn syrup
2 tablespoons butter or margarine
1/2 cup evaporated milk
1/4 cup milk
Dash of salt
1 teaspoon vanilla

Butter cooking pan (9 × 5 inches) thoroughly before starting. Combine sugars, syrup, butter or margarine, milks, and salt. Cook over medium heat, stirring constantly until mixture boils. Lower heat and continue to cook to 238°, or soft-ball stage, stirring often to prevent scorching. Remove from heat, add vanilla, but do not stir until cooled to lukewarm. Beat until glossy. Pour into buttered pan. When firm, cut into squares. *Makes about 30 pieces.*

Caramel Corn

2 cups packed brown sugar
1/2 cup light corn syrup
1 cup butter or margarine
1 teaspoon salt
1/2 teaspoon baking soda
1 teaspoon vanilla
6 quarts popped corn

Combine sugar, syrup, butter or margarine, and salt in heavy saucepan. Bring to boil, stirring constantly over medium heat until mixture reaches 260° on candy thermometer, or hard-ball stage. Remove from heat; stir in baking soda and vanilla. Pour over popped corn and stir until all kernels are well coated. Spread corn out on two buttered cookie sheets. Bake in 200° oven for 1 hour, stirring well after first 30 minutes. Remove from oven and spread out on waxed paper. Let cool completely. *Makes about 6¹/₂ quarts.*

Pralines

2 cups sugar
³/₄ teaspoon baking soda
1 cup light cream or whole milk
1¹/₂ tablespoons butter or margarine
2 cups pecan halves

Combine sugar and baking soda; stir in cream or milk. Bring to boil over medium heat, stirring constantly. Reduce heat, continue to cook, and stir until mixture reaches soft-ball stage, or 234° on the candy thermometer. Mixture will caramelize slightly. Remove from heat and add butter or margarine. Stir in pecans and beat until thick. Drop from tablespoon onto waxed paper. *Makes about 30 candies.*

TAFFY PULL

When we were growing up, most of the candy Troll and I ever laid hands on was homemade. Mom was a terrible candymaker. Her fudge practically had to be gouged off the plate with a jackhammer. Her divinity turned out as little white puddles. Eventually, my sister took over the candymaking, using Aunt Verda's and Aunt Gladys's never-fail recipes, which somehow had always failed with Mom. Once Mom and Troll made some taffy, and even today I am moved to glee at recalling the scene. The hot taffy was dumped out in a glob on the table, and Mom and Troll grabbed it up and started pulling it while it was still too hot. It began to stick to their fingers. The only way they could get it off one set of fingers was to pull it off with the other set of fingers, and then the taffy would stick to those fingers. Unable to release the taffy, the two of them bounded about the kitchen, yelling and cursing, knocking over chairs, smashing dishes, terrifying the dog and cat, and pulling the smoldering taffy faster than the eye could follow. I had never seen taffy pulled before and thought this must be the way it was done. If I had known taffy pulling would be so entertaining, I'd have sold tickets for the performance to my friends, but only to those who had grown up around loggers or were otherwise immune to rough language. I certainly wouldn't want to be responsible for stunting a sensitive kid's growth by exposing him to a taffy pull.

Taffy

  1 cup light corn syrup
  $1/2$ cup sugar
  1 tablespoon cider vinegar
  1 teaspoon butter or margarine
  $1/2$ teaspoon vanilla

Combine all ingredients except vanilla in heavy saucepan and boil until mixture reaches 260° on candy thermometer, or hard-ball stage. Remove from heat and add vanilla. Pour onto lightly buttered platter. Butter hands before starting to pull taffy. When candy is cool enough to handle, and you can be fooled by thinking it is, start pulling the taffy by carefully stretching one end with one hand while holding the other end in the other hand; then fold it back upon itself. Continue to do this until the candy is light and porous. Roll into a long rope, then cut into bite-size pieces.

OTHER DESSERTS
AND PIES

Huckleberry Slump

2 1/2 cups huckleberries
1/2 cup sugar
Dash of salt
1 cup water
1 tablespoon lemon juice
1 cup sifted flour
2 tablespoons sugar
2 teaspoons baking powder
1/4 teaspoon salt
1 tablespoon butter or margarine
1/2 cup milk

Bring berries, 1/2 cup sugar, salt, and water to a boil; cover and simmer 5 minutes. Add lemon juice and return to a boil.

Sift together the dry ingredients. Cut in butter or margarine until mixture resembles coarse meal. Add milk all at once and stir only until flour is dampened. Approximating ⅙ of the amount, drop batter from serving spoon into bubbling berry mixture, making 6 dumplings. Cover tightly and cook over low heat for 10 minutes without lifting lid. Serve dumplings hot with huckleberry sauce over them. *Serves 6.*

Gram's Cherry Cobbler

BATTER:

½ cup butter or margarine
1 cup flour
½ cup sugar
2 teaspoons baking powder
¾ cup milk

FILLING:

1 pint pie cherries, pitted
¾ cup sugar
2 tablespoons flour

Preheat oven to 350°. Place butter or margarine in pan (8 × 8 inches) and let melt in oven. Mix well 1 cup flour, ½ cup sugar, 2 teaspoons baking powder, and ¾ cup milk and pour over slightly cooled butter/margarine; do not mix together.

Mix cherries, sugar, and flour together. Spoon gently over batter layer without mixing layers. Bake at 350° for 40 to 50 minutes or until brown. Crust will form on top and fruit will be on the bottom. *Serves 6.*

Rhubarb Cobbler

BATTER:

1 cup flour
³/₄ cup oatmeal
1 teaspoon cinnamon
1 cup packed brown sugar
¹/₂ cup butter or margarine, melted

FILLING:

1 cup water
1 cup sugar
3 tablespoons cornstarch
1 tablespoon vanilla
4 cups rhubarb, thinly sliced

Mix batter ingredients together and press half of mixture into pan (8 × 8 inches). Cook water, sugar, cornstarch, and vanilla together until thick; then add rhubarb. Spread over first mixture and top with remaining half of batter. Bake at 350° for 1 hour. *Serves 6.*

Burnt Creme

1 pint whipping cream
4 egg yolks
¹/₂ cup sugar
2 teaspoons vanilla
Sugar for sprinkling

Heat cream over low heat until bubbles form around edge of pan. Beat egg yolks and sugar together until thick and yellow. Beating constantly, pour cream in steady stream into egg mixture. Add vanilla and pour into custard cups. Place custard cups in baking pan that has from ½ to 1 inch boiling water in the bottom. Bake at 350° for 45 minutes. Remove from water and chill about 2 hours. Sprinkle with sugar and place under broiler until sugar topping is medium brown. Refrigerate until served. *Makes 6 servings.*

Custard

3 cups milk
3 eggs, slightly beaten
½ cup sugar
Pinch of salt
1 teaspoon vanilla
Nutmeg

Scald milk and cool. Add milk, eggs, sugar, salt, and vanilla. Pour into 6 custard cups and sprinkle with nutmeg. Set cups in baking pan and pour boiling water to within an inch of tops of cups. Bake at 325° for 45 minutes to 1 hour or until knife inserted in center comes out clean. *Makes 6 servings.*

Apple Pudding

1 cup sugar
½ cup butter or margarine

1 egg
4 medium tart apples, peeled and sliced thin
¼ cup chopped walnuts
1 cup flour
1 teaspoon baking soda
Dash of salt
½ teaspoon nutmeg
½ teaspoon cinnamon
1 teaspoon vanilla

Cream sugar and butter or margarine; blend in egg. Stir in apples and walnuts. Sift flour, baking soda, and spices together; add to the mixture. Add vanilla. Mix well. Bake in greased pan (9 × 9 inches) in 375° oven for 30 to 40 minutes, or until done. Serve with thick cream or ice cream. *Makes 9 servings.*

Upside-Down Pudding

1¼ cups sugar
2 tablespoons butter or margarine
1 cup sifted flour
Dash of salt
1 teaspoon baking powder
¾ cup milk
2 cups sliced canned fruit (peaches,
    pineapple, fruit cocktail)
½ cup fruit juice

Cream 1 cup sugar with butter or margarine. Add dry ingredients alternately with milk. Pour into greased pan (9 × 9 inches). Heat fruit, fruit juice, and remaining ¼ cup sugar to boiling and pour over batter. Bake for 30 minutes at 350°. Serve with cream or ice cream. *Serves 6.*

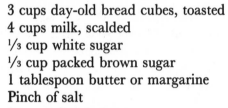

Dad's Bread Pudding

3 cups day-old bread cubes, toasted
4 cups milk, scalded
1/3 cup white sugar
1/3 cup packed brown sugar
1 tablespoon butter or margarine
Pinch of salt
3 eggs, slightly beaten
2 teaspoons vanilla
1/2 cup seedless raisins
Nutmeg

Soak bread cubes in scalded milk for a few minutes. Add rest of ingredients, except nutmeg, and mix thoroughly, keeping bread cubes as whole as possible. Pour into buttered pan (9 × 9 inches) and sprinkle with nutmeg. Set pudding in larger pan and pour boiling water around it. Bake at 325° for 1 hour or until knife inserted in center comes out clean. *Serves 6.*

Butterscotch Pudding

2 tablespoons cornstarch
2 tablespoons flour

2 tablespoons butter or margarine
1 cup packed brown sugar
2 eggs, beaten
2 cups milk
1 teaspoon vanilla

Combine all ingredients except vanilla and cook in the top of a double boiler, stirring until mixture boils and is thick and creamy. Remove from heat and stir in vanilla. *Serves 4.*

Chocolate Pudding

⅓ cup cocoa
1¼ cups sugar
⅓ cup cornstarch
¼ teaspoon salt
3 cups milk
3 tablespoons butter or margarine
¼ cup rum
Pie shell (optional)
1 cup whipping cream
Sugar and vanilla for whipped cream

Combine cocoa, 1¼ cups sugar, cornstarch, and salt in medium saucepan. Blend in milk, stirring until smooth. Cook over medium heat, stirring constantly, until mixture comes to a boil. Boil and stir 1 minute. Remove from heat; add butter or margarine and rum. Stir well. Pour into 6 dishes or a baked 9-inch pie shell. Chill until firm. Serve with whipped cream flavored with 1 to 2 tablespoons sugar and ½ teaspoon vanilla. *Serves 6.*

Glorified Rice

1 cup whipping cream
½ cup sugar
1 teaspoon vanilla
1 cup cold cooked rice
1 cup pineapple tidbits, drained

Whip cream and sweeten with sugar; add vanilla. Combine rice and pineapple and fold in whipped cream. Refrigerate. *Serves 4.*

Hot Fudge Sauce

2 cups sugar
1 heaping tablespoon flour
12 tablespoons cocoa
8 tablespoons butter or margarine
1 can (12 ounces) evaporated milk
1 teaspoon vanilla
½ teaspoon salt

Mix sugar, flour, and cocoa until free of lumps before adding milk. Add half the butter or margarine (4 tablespoons) and milk. In flat-bottom pan, boil for 1 minute, stirring constantly from bottom of pan to keep mixture from burning. Remove from heat. Add vanilla, salt, and remaining butter or margarine. Store in refrigerator. Heat before serving over ice cream. *Makes 1 quart.*

Huckleberry Sauce

Delicious served over cake or ice cream.

$^1/_2$ cup sugar
2 tablespoons cornstarch
$^1/_2$ cup cold water
2 cups huckleberries

Combine sugar and cornstarch. Add cold water and stir until smooth. Add huckleberries, bring to a boil, and cook until clear. Cool and serve over ice cream or cake. *Makes approximately 2$^1/_2$ cups.*

Orange Sauce

This is an ideal topping for a slice of white or angel food cake.

2 eggs or 5 egg yolks, slightly beaten
Grated rind of 1 orange
1 cup orange juice
2 tablespoons flour
2 tablespoons lemon juice
$^3/_4$ cup sugar
Pinch of salt
1 pint whipping cream

Combine all of the ingredients, except for whipping cream, in the top of a double boiler and cook until thick, stirring constantly. Cool and store in refrigerator until needed. Just before serving, whip the cream and fold into chilled mixture. *Makes about 4 cups.*

Chocolate Silk Pie

Very rich, but very good!

²/₃ cup butter or margarine
1 cup sugar
2 1-ounce squares unsweetened chocolate,
    melted and cooled
1 teaspoon vanilla
2 extra-large eggs or 3 smaller eggs
1 baked 9-inch pie shell

TOPPING:

1 cup whipping cream
2 tablespoons sugar
¹/₂ teaspoon vanilla
Grated chocolate bar

Beat butter or margarine with a mixer until fluffy. Gradually beat in sugar until dissolved. Add melted chocolate and vanilla. Add 1 egg at a time, beating on medium speed for 5 minutes after adding each egg, until very fluffy. Pour into pie shell and chill 3–5 hours. Top with sweetened whipped cream and trim with grated chocolate bar. *Serves 9.*

Vanilla Cream Pie

2 egg yolks
1 tablespoon flour
1 tablespoon cornstarch
1 cup whole milk
$\frac{1}{3}$ cup white sugar (or more for sweeter pie)
4 tablespoons packed brown sugar
Pinch of salt
1 teaspoon butter or margarine
1 cup evaporated milk
1 teaspoon vanilla
1 baked 8-inch pie shell
Meringue (see p. 227)
$\frac{1}{2}$ pint whipping cream (optional) sweetened with
   2 tablespoons sugar and $\frac{1}{2}$ teaspoon vanilla

Beat egg yolks until fluffy. Add flour and cornstarch, which have been mixed with $\frac{1}{4}$ cup whole milk and beat well. Add sugars, salt, butter or margarine, remainder of whole milk, and evaporated milk. Mix well. Cook in the top of a double boiler, stirring often, until thickened. Remove from heat and add vanilla. Pour into baked shell. Cover with meringue, or chill and serve with sweetened whipped cream. *Serves 6.*

Banana Cream Pie

Make recipe for Vanilla Cream Pie and fold in 2 sliced bananas.

Coconut Cream Pie

Make recipe for Vanilla Cream Pie and fold in $\frac{1}{2}$ cup coconut. If using meringue, sprinkle lightly with coconut before baking.

Pineapple Cream Pie

Make recipe for Vanilla Cream Pie and fold in 1 can (6½ ounces) crushed pineapple that has been thoroughly drained.

Raisin Sour Cream Pie

> ¾ cup sugar
> 2 tablespoons cornstarch
> ¼ teaspoon salt
> 2 eggs, beaten
> 2 cups sour cream
> 1 cup seedless raisins
> 2 tablespoons lemon juice
> 1 baked 9-inch pie shell

In top of double boiler, blend together sugar, cornstarch, and salt. Combine with beaten eggs, 1½ cups sour cream, raisins, and lemon juice. Cook and stir over hot water until thick. Pour into baked pie shell. When cool, top with remaining ½ cup sour cream. Chill several hours. *Serves 6.*

Custard Pie

> 1 unbaked 9-inch deep-dish pie shell
> 4 eggs
> ⅔ cup sugar
> ¼ teaspoon salt
> 1½ cups milk, scalded

1 cup light cream, scalded
1 teaspoon vanilla
1/2 teaspoon nutmeg

Chill pie shell. Beat eggs slightly, then beat in remaining ingredients, except for nutmeg. Pour into well-chilled pie shell. Sprinkle with nutmeg. Bake at 400° for 25 to 35 minutes, or until a knife inserted an inch from edge of shell comes out clean. *Serves 6.*

Strawberry Pie

3 pints strawberries, hulled and washed
1 cup sugar
3 1/2 tablespoons cornstarch
1/2 cup water
1 tablespoon butter or margarine
Red food coloring (optional)
1 baked 9-inch pie shell
1/2 pint whipping cream sweetened with
    2 tablespoons sugar and 1/2 teaspoon vanilla

Mash 1 pint strawberries or enough to make 1 cup mashed berries. Mix together sugar and cornstarch; stir in water and mashed berries. Cook over medium heat, stirring until mixture boils. Continue boiling for 2 minutes. Remove from heat. Stir in butter or margarine and cool. Add a few drops red food coloring. Put remaining berries in pie shell and pour cooked, cooled mixture on top. Chill. Serve with sweetened whipped cream. *Serves 6.*

Mom's Apple Pie

7 large tart (and, if possible, green) apples
2 tablespoons flour
³/₄ cup white sugar
¹/₃ cup packed brown sugar
1 teaspoon cinnamon
¹/₂ teaspoon nutmeg
2 tablespoons butter or margarine
Dough for 2-crust pie (see pp. 227–228)
Evaporated milk
2 tablespoons sugar

Peel and slice apples. Mix dry ingredients (except 2 table-spoons sugar) and stir through the apples. Pour apple mixture into pastry-lined 9-inch pie pan and dot with butter or margarine. Add top crust, crimp edges, and prick with fork. Brush with evaporated milk and sprinkle with 2 tablespoons sugar. Bake at 400° for 20 minutes; lower heat to 350° and bake for 25 to 30 minutes, or until apples are tender. *Serves 6.*

Sour Cream Apple Pie

5 large tart apples
1 unbaked 9-inch pie shell
1 tablespoon lemon juice
³/₄ cup sugar
¹/₃ cup flour
¹/₄ teaspoon salt
1 teaspoon cinnamon
¹/₄ teaspoon nutmeg

¼ cup butter or margarine
½ cup sour cream

Peel and cut apples into thick slices. Arrange apples in overlapping rows in pastry-lined pan. Sprinkle with lemon juice. Combine sugar, flour, salt, cinnamon, and nutmeg. Cut in butter or margarine until crumbly. Sprinkle over apples. Spread sour cream over top. Bake at 400° for 25 minutes; reduce heat to 350° and bake until apples are tender, about 20 to 25 minutes longer. *Serves 6.*

Mom's Dewberry Pie

In the summer we spent lots of time picking dewberries in the woods near our home. The reward was dewberry pie and no matter how prickly the thorns, it was worth it.

1 cup sugar
¼ cup flour
Dash of salt
3 cups dewberries
Dough for 2-crust pie (see pp. 227–228)
2 tablespoons butter or margarine
2 tablespoons cold water

Mix sugar, flour, and salt together and stir gently through berries. Pour into pastry-lined 9-inch pie pan. Dot with butter or margarine and sprinkle with water. Cover with top crust, seal, crimp edges, and prick top with fork. Bake at 450° for 10 minutes, reduce heat to 375°, and bake about 30 minutes longer until crust is golden brown and juice is bubbling. *Serves 6.*

Old Woodcutter's Elderberry-Apple Pie

Be sure to use only powder-blue elderberries; red or shiny black elderberries are poisonous.

Dough for 2-crust pie (see pp. 227–228)
2 cups powder-blue elderberries
2 cups peeled and chopped tart apples
1 cup sugar
3 tablespoons tapioca
Pinch of salt
2 tablespoons butter or margarine
Evaporated milk
2 tablespoons sugar

Line 9-inch pie pan with pie crust. Be sure all stems are removed from the elderberries. Mix cleaned elderberries, apples, sugar, tapioca, and salt; pour into pie shell. Dot with butter or margarine. Cover with top crust and flute edges. Prick with fork. Brush crust with evaporated milk and sprinkle with sugar. Bake at 400° for 35 to 40 minutes. *Serves 6.*

Vic's Gooseberry Pie

4 cups gooseberries
1 egg, beaten
1 cup white sugar
¼ cup packed brown sugar
2 tablespoons flour

Dough for 2-crust pie (see pp. 227–228)
Evaporated milk
2 tablespoons sugar

Look gooseberries over carefully, wash, and drain. Combine egg, sugars, and flour; stir in gooseberries. Pour into pastry-lined 9-inch pie pan, cover with top crust, crimp edges, and prick with fork. Brush with evaporated milk and sprinkle with sugar. Bake at 425° for 35 to 40 minutes, or until crust is golden brown. *Serves 6.*

Favorite Huckleberry Cream Pie

Cousin Bud's idea of gourmet eating is peanut butter on toast, but his favorite huckleberry pie is our favorite, too.

1 package (8 ounces) cream cheese
1 cup powdered sugar
1 teaspoon vanilla
1 cup cream, whipped
1 baked 9-inch pie shell

Cream the cream cheese, powdered sugar, and vanilla. Gently fold in the whipped cream. Spread on bottom and up sides of pie shell.

3 cups huckleberries
1 cup sugar
¼ cup flour
Dash of salt
1 tablespoon lemon juice

Cook above ingredients over low heat until they come to a boil and thicken. Cool and spread over cream cheese layer. Refrigerate. *Very rich—serves 8.*

Huckleberry Pie

  2 teaspoons lemon juice
  4 cups huckleberries
  3 tablespoons flour
  1 cup sugar
  Dough for 2-crust pie (see pp. 227–228)
  2 tablespoons butter or margarine

Mix lemon juice with huckleberries. Combine flour and sugar; stir through berries. Pour into crust, dot with butter or margarine, and cover with top crust. Crimp edges and prick with fork. Bake at 425° for 15 minutes; lower heat to 350° and bake for 30 minutes longer, or until crust is golden brown and juice bubbles. *Serves 6.*

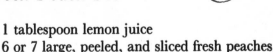

Fresh Peach Pie

  1 tablespoon lemon juice
  6 or 7 large, peeled, and sliced fresh peaches

1/2 cup white sugar
1/4 cup packed brown sugar
3 tablespoons flour
Dough for 2-crust pie (see pp. 227–228)
2 tablespoons butter or margarine
Evaporated milk
2 tablespoons white sugar

Sprinkle lemon juice over peaches. Mix sugars and flour together and mix gently through peaches. Pour into 9-inch pie crust and dot with butter or margarine. Cover with top crust, crimp edges, and prick top with fork. Brush top crust with evaporated milk and sprinkle lightly with sugar. Bake at 425° for 15 minutes; lower heat to 350° and bake for 35 minutes more, or until crust is golden brown. *Serves 6.*

Rhubarb Cream Pie

Dough for 2-crust pie (see pp. 227–228)
3 cups rhubarb, chopped
2 eggs, slightly beaten
1 1/2 cups sugar
3 tablespoons flour
1 tablespoon butter or margarine
1 teaspoon nutmeg

Place rhubarb in 9-inch pie shell. Combine other ingredients and pour over rhubarb. Cover with top crust, flute edges, and prick top with fork. Bake at 425° for 1 hour. *Serves 6.*

Rhubarb Custard Pie

3 cups diced rhubarb
1½ cups sugar
3 egg yolks
2 tablespoons butter or margarine
2 tablespoons flour
Few drops of red food coloring
1 baked 9-inch pie shell
Meringue (see p. 227)

Mix first six ingredients and cook slowly until thickened, stirring all the time. Pour into baked pie shell. Cover with meringue. *Serves 6.*

Rhubarb-Strawberry Pie

¼ cup flour
1 cup sugar
Dash of salt
3 cups sliced fresh rhubarb
2 cups sliced fresh strawberries
Dough for 2-crust pie (see pp. 227–228)
2 tablespoons powdered strawberry
   Jell-O

Mix flour, sugar, and salt with the rhubarb and strawberries. Pour into 9-inch crust and sprinkle with Jell-O. Cover with top crust, crimp edges, and prick top with fork. Bake at 450° for 10 minutes; lower heat to 350° and bake for 50 minutes, or until crust is golden brown. *Serves 6.*

Angel Pecan Pie

1 cup Ritz crackers or white soda crackers
2 egg whites
1 cup sugar
1 teaspoon vanilla
1 cup plus ¼ cup broken pecans or walnuts
1 pint whipping cream sweetened with
  ¼ cup sugar and 1 teaspoon vanilla

Break the crackers into 5 or 6 pieces each. Do not crush them. Beat egg whites stiff, adding 1 cup sugar gradually, then add vanilla. Fold in cracker pieces and 1 cup nuts. Bake in greased 9-inch pie pan at 350° for 30 minutes. Cool and top with sweetened whipped cream. Sprinkle ¼ cup chopped nuts on top. *Serves 6.*

Pecan Pie

This pie is known as Washington Nut Pie when it is made with walnuts instead of pecans.

1 cup packed dark brown sugar
½ cup butter or margarine
1 cup light corn syrup
Dash of salt
1½ teaspoons vanilla
3 eggs, slightly beaten
1½ cups pecans (or walnuts)
1 unbaked 9-inch pie shell

Combine brown sugar, butter or margarine, corn syrup, salt, and vanilla. Stir until blended. Stir in eggs. Fold in nuts and pour into pie shell. Bake at 375° for 40 to 50 minutes, or until pie is set. *Serves 8.*

Lemon Meringue Pie

FILLING:

1½ cups sugar
½ cup cornstarch
Dash of salt
2½ cups water
4 egg yolks
2 tablespoons butter or margarine
½ cup fresh lemon juice
1 tablespoon grated lemon rind
1 baked 9-inch pie shell

MERINGUE:

4 egg whites
8 tablespoons sugar

Combine sugar, cornstarch, and salt; gradually stir in water. Cook over low heat, stirring constantly, until mixture starts to thicken. Beat egg yolks, and gradually pour a small amount of hot mixture into them. Stir and pour egg mixture back into pan. Return to heat and continue cooking and stirring until mixture comes to a boil. Cook until thick. Remove from heat and add butter or margarine, lemon juice, and rind. Stir well and pour into baked pie shell. Cover while warm with meringue. See following page for meringue baking method, but amounts given here are better for this pie. *Serves 6.*

Meringue

3 egg whites
¼ teaspoon salt
Pinch of cream of tartar
6 tablespoons sugar

Have egg whites at room temperature. Add salt and cream of
tartar. Beat until egg whites are frothy, then add 1 tablespoon
sugar at a time, sprinkling it gently over the whites. Continue
to beat until stiff peaks form when your beater is raised. Spread
on pie, being sure to touch the crust all the way around and
mound in the center. Bake at 400° for 8 minutes, or until
golden brown. Shut off oven, but leave door partially open
until pie cools to warm. *Makes enough meringue for one 8- or 9-
inch pie.*

Pie Crust

3 cups flour
1 teaspoon salt
¼ teaspoon baking powder
1 cup cold vegetable shortening
Ice-cold water

Combine flour, salt, and baking powder. Cut in shortening
with pastry blender until mixture resembles coarse cornmeal.
Gradually sprinkle on small amounts of cold water, stirring
with fork until dough is moist enough to hold together. If
recipe calls for baked pie crust, bake at 425° for 12 to 15

minutes, or until golden brown. *Makes one 9-inch double-crust pie plus one 9-inch single shell (3 crusts in all).*

Milk Pie Crust

3 cups flour
1 teaspoon salt
1 teaspoon sugar
1 cup plus 2 tablespoons vegetable shortening
Cold milk

Mix dry ingredients. Cut in shortening until mixture resembles coarse cornmeal. Add cold milk, a little at a time, stirring with a fork, until dough holds together. If recipe calls for baked pie crust, bake at 425° for 12 to 15 minutes, or until golden brown. *Makes enough dough for one 9-inch double-crust pie and one 9-inch single pie shell (3 crusts in all).*

Uncle Ralph's Lard Pie Crust

3 cups flour
1/2 teaspoon baking powder
1 teaspoon salt
3/4 cup lard
Cold water

Mix flour, baking powder, and salt. Blend in lard until mixture resembles coarse crumbs. Add cold water, a little at a time, until dough holds together. If recipe calls for baked pie crust, bake at 425° for 12 to 15 minutes, or until golden brown. *Makes one 9-inch double-crust and one 9-inch single pie shell (3 crusts in all).*

ODDS AND ENDS

Kippered Cherries

Pit as many sour cherries as you wish to use. This must be done by pinching out the seeds with your fingers or extracting them with a hand pitter that you feed the cherries into. Cherries must have a good shape.

Put the pitted cherries into a bowl or crock and cover with cider vinegar. Cover the bowl and let it stand for 3 days. Then drain and measure the cherries. Add 1 cup sugar to each cup fruit, and allow to stand for 3 more days. Be sure to stir well each day so that the sugar melts completely and permeates the fruit. Put ½ stick cinnamon into each freshly washed, sterilized pint jar. Add the sugared fruit and seal. No cooking or processing of any kind. These cherries will keep indefinitely if stored in a cool place.

Brandied Plums

4 pounds large ripe plums
1 quart best-quality brandy
6 cups sugar

Select the largest possible plums. They should be soft and quite ripe. Wipe each plum clean with a damp cloth, then prick in several places with the tines of a fork. Place plums in a large glass jar or a stoneware crock and pour the brandy over them. Cover with several thicknesses of cheesecloth and tie it in place with string or secure with a large rubber band. Let stand in a cool, dry, and dark place for 10 days.

Put sugar in a large pan and pour the plums and brandy over it. When the juices from the fruit have saturated the sugar, you are ready to put the pan on the stove. Cook over low heat until the sugar dissolves, stirring often. Then let boil gently for 25 to 30 minutes, stirring occasionally at first, then quite often to prevent scorching. Remove from heat and ladle into hot sterilized jars and seal. *Makes about 6 pint jars.*

Huckleberry Syrup

Cook approximately 3 quarts huckleberries in small amount of water until soft. Strain juice through several layers of cheesecloth to obtain the juice needed to make this recipe.

4 cups huckleberry juice
2 cups sugar
2 cups light corn syrup

Measure 4 cups berry juice into saucepan. Stir in sugar and corn syrup. Bring to a full rolling boil. Remove from heat; skim if necessary. Pour immediately into hot sterilized jars. Adjust lids; process in boiling-water bath 10 minutes for pints or quarts. *Makes 7 or 8 cups.*

Huckleberry Liqueur

This recipe works equally well with almost any tart berry and is especially good with pie cherries.

    1 bottle (750 milliliters) vodka
    1 pound cube sugar
    Huckleberries

Divide vodka between two 750-milliliter liquor bottles. Drop ½ pound sugar cubes into neck of each bottle. Drop berries into bottle up to where the neck begins to taper. Place tops on loosely. Set aside for 7 days at room temperature. Store for a month with the tops loose. Be sure to upend the bottles, after first tightening the tops, a couple of times each day until the sugar is dissolved. Do not shake the bottles. Pour liquor through cheesecloth and return liquor to bottles. Put tops on tight; it is now ready to use. Store in cool place. *Makes 2 750-milliliter bottles.*

*I*f making homemade wine, these recipes can be used as they are written. They are old-time recipes, however. A better grade of wine can be produced if a fermentation lock or water seal is used according to directions. A fermentation lock or water seal is a small plastic device that is filled to a prescribed level with water. Gas formed during fermentation pushes through the water in the form of bubbles but airborne wild yeasts and bacteria are kept out. The fermentation lock also tells when fermentation has stopped. Campden tablets play an important role in wine making, as they destroy wild yeasts and bacteria, allowing added yeasts to work more efficiently. All wine-making supplies and instructions can be purchased at a wine-making supply shop. Sterilizing utensils and clean fruit are essential. Good luck! Hic!

(The yield for wine is approximately 4 quarts to each gallon of juice.)

Blackberry Wine

Pour 2 quarts water over each gallon of blackberries and let stand 3 days. At end of that time, press out juice. For each gallon of juice, add 3 pounds sugar and ½ ounce yeast and stir until dissolved. Set aside for 3 more days. Strain. Put in keg and apply water seal. Bottle in December.

Chokecherry Wine

   1 gallon cleaned and crushed chokecherries
   1 gallon boiling water
   4 pounds sugar
   Dry yeast
   1 slice whole wheat bread

Pour boiling water over chokecherries and let stand for 24 hours or more. Strain juice, measure, and place in crock. For each gallon of juice, add 4 pounds sugar. Stir well and add ½ package dry yeast (whatever the amount of juice). Place 1 slice whole wheat bread on top and let stand 2 weeks in covered crock. Siphon wine into gallon jugs. Put an ordinary, fairly large balloon on top. Let the yeast process continue working. The wine should age for 1 year before being corked.

Dandelion Wine

This makes a beautiful yellow wine. We always planned to use it for Christmas, but it was sampled so much to see if it was ready, there was never any left for the holidays.

2 gallons dandelion blossoms
16 cups white sugar
2 gallons boiling water
3 lemons, sliced
3 oranges, sliced
1 pound white raisins
2 yeast cakes

Remove all stems and green from the dandelion blossoms and rinse with cool water. Place in large crock. Pour sugar on the blossoms and then pour the boiling water over all. Stir. Cool to lukewarm. Add sliced lemons, oranges, white raisins, and yeast cakes. Stir well and cover with cheesecloth. Let stand for 48 hours. Strain and let liquid set for 5 days covered with cheesecloth. Strain again and let ferment in warm spot until fermentation stops. Bottle. Try not to use for 6 months!

Elderberry Wine

Please note that the red and shiny black elderberries are poisonous; use only the powder-blue elderberries. Also, be sure to get all the little twigs off the berries. Even one twig will spoil the wine.

Pour 1 gallon boiling water over each gallon ripe powder-blue elderberries. Stir well and let stand quietly for a day. Press out juice, squeezing berries to remove all of the juice. For each gallon of juice, add 3 pounds sugar, ³⁄₄ ounce powdered cloves, and 1 ounce ground ginger. Boil together for 20 minutes, skimming all the time. Cool to lukewarm; put in crock with 1 yeast cake. In 3 or 4 days water-seal and let stand 3 months before bottling.

Huckleberry Wine

Pour 1 gallon boiling water over every gallon crushed huckleberries and let stand in crock 24 hours. Stir often, and after 24 hours, strain. Dissolve 2 pounds sugar in each gallon juice, turn into clean cask, and water seal. When finished fermenting, remove water seal, and mix in 4 well-beaten egg whites for every 5 gallons wine. Bung up tightly and let stand 3 months. Bottle.

Rhubarb W̶̶

8 pounds finely s̶̶ ̶rb
8 quarts boiling wa̶̶
2 whole lemons, finely
4 teaspoons almond extr̶̶
8 pounds sugar
2 packages dry yeast, dissolv̶̶ ̶ ¹/₂ cup
   warm water
2 envelopes unflavored gelatin,
   dissolved in ¹/₂ cup warm water

Combine rhubarb, boiling water, lemons, and almond extract.
Let stand 3 days. Strain mixture. Add sugar and yeast; let
stand 2 days. Mix in softened gelatin; let stand for 12 days.
Bottle and cork.

Chokecherry Jam

Remove stems from chokecherries and wash well. Add 1 cup
water for every 4 cups fruit. Place over low heat and simmer
until fruit is very soft, stirring occasionally. Rub pulp through
medium sieve, measure, and add equal amount of sugar. Place
over medium heat and stir until sugar is dissolved. Bring to
a full rolling boil and cook until mixture sheets on a spoon,
or 220°. Seal in hot sterilized jars and process in boiling-water
bath for 5 minutes. *Three cups of pulp will make approximately 3
half-pints jam.*

Chokecherry Jelly

    5 cups chokecherry juice
    ½ cup lemon juice
    1 package powdered pectin
    5½ cups sugar

Boil chokecherry juice, lemon juice, and pectin for 3 minutes; add sugar and stir well. Cook until juice coats a spoon, about 5 to 8 minutes. Pour into hot sterilized jars and seal. *Makes 6 half-pints (or 6 cups).*

Corncob Jelly

This jelly tastes very much like honey.

    12 corncobs from which corn
       has been cut
    4 cups water
    1 box powdered pectin
    4 cups sugar

Boil corncobs and water for 10 minutes. Strain and measure 3 cups juice. Water may be added to make the 3 cups. Add pectin to juice, bring to a boil, and add sugar. Bring to a boil again, skim, put in hot sterilized jars, and seal. *Makes 4 half-pints.*

Clover Honey

100 purple clover blossoms
3 cups water
10 cups sugar
1 teaspoon alum

Clean clover blossoms, cover with water, and boil for 3 minutes. Strain and keep the liquid, adding more water, if necessary, to make 3 cups. Bring to boil; add sugar and alum. Let boil for 5 minutes. Put in hot sterilized jars and seal. *Makes 4 half-pints.*

Elderberry or Blackberry Jam

Same directions for both kinds of jam. Use only powder-blue elderberries; the red and shiny black elderberries are poisonous.

4 cups powder-blue elderberries or blackberries
3 cups sugar

If the elderberries are tart, use a scant cup sugar to 1 cup fruit. Combine the berries with the sugar and stir. Cook over low heat until the sugar is dissolved. Simmer and stir from the bottom to keep the berries from sticking. Cook until a small amount dropped on a plate will stay in place. Pour into hot sterilized jars and process in boiling water for 5 minutes. *Makes 3 half-pints.*

*I*n early summer we would start looking for the elderberry bushes with the most clusters of blossoms in anticipation of elderberry jam, jelly, and pies. We also made elderberry wine (see p. 234) in fairly large quantities, always telling friends that it was really for the holidays. It never lasted until the holidays.

In late fall after the first frost, we would go up Trestle Creek to pick the clusters of berries. It didn't take long to pick them, but the tedious job was getting all the little stems off. This was Pat's and my job. It seemed like it took forever. One batch of elderberry wine we made had a strong taste and Gram was sure it was because some stems were left on. Not only was the taste strong, this wine felled the hardiest and most hardened of drinkers. I wasn't sure if it was the stems or the pound of raisins Gram accidentally put in the wine.

An easier way to get the stems off is to put the berries in paper sacks in the freezer and let them freeze, then shake the bags. Most of the stems will fall off.

Elderberry Jelly

Use only powder-blue elderberries; the red and shiny black elderberries are poisonous.

6 cups elderberry juice made from powder-blue elderberries
1/2 cup lemon juice
2 boxes powdered pectin
7 cups sugar

Combine juices and pectin. Bring to a hard boil and add sugar. Boil hard for 2 minutes. Skim off foam. Pour into hot sterilized jars and seal. *Makes 7 half-pints.*

Huckleberry Jam

4½ cups crushed huckleberries
7 cups sugar
2 tablespoons lemon juice
2 pouches (3 ounces) liquid pectin

Measure berries, sugar, and lemon juice into a large pan and stir well. Bring to a rolling boil for 1 minute, stirring constantly. Remove from heat and stir in liquid pectin. Stir and skim off foam for several minutes. Ladle into hot sterilized jars and adjust lids. Process in boiling water for 10 minutes to assure seal. *Makes approximately 4 pints.*

Mom's Cracklings

When we butchered a pig in the fall, the lard was always rendered out of the fat. The fat was cut off the pig and cut up into small pieces. It was then put in a very large pan, either in the oven or on top of the stove. It was cooked for quite a long time and as the melted fat rose to the top, it was skimmed off and put in jars or crocks. When all the fat was rendered, the cracklings were left. We ate them with salt and pepper and everyone told us how delicious they were. We weren't too smart. We were convinced that the fried pig tail was the best part of the pig so naturally Pat and I would fight for the pig tail.

WHATCHAGOT STEW

*T*roll finally agreed that I could have my own section of recipes at the end of the book, where it could be easily quarantined. I have called this section "Whatchagot Stew," because I have, in addition to my own recipes, various choice leftovers that I wanted to toss in somewhere. If you find it a bit chaotic, that is my intent. We began with chaos and we shall end with chaos.

WILD, WILD DINNERS

*A*nyone involved with hunting and fishing sooner or later finds himself at what is appropriately named a "wild dinner." In its simplest state, a wild dinner is also known as an "empty-the-freezer dinner." This usually occurs in April or about the beginning of fishing season. The sportsman empties all the wild game from his freezer, thaws it out, and, using his favorite recipes, cooks it all up into one gigantic meal for his friends and neighbors and anyone else who happens by. The variety of empty-the-freezer meals is often enormous—elk steak cooked in a gravy of dried onion soup and canned celery soup; venison meatballs cooked in a gravy of dried onion soup and canned celery soup; grouse, quail, pheasant, dove cooked in a gravy of dried onion soup and canned celery soup. (Recipe for onion-and-celery-soup gravy shows up somewhere later on.)

The true wild dinner is usually a project of a sportsmen's club. All the members bring dishes as exotic as possible, and you have the opportunity to taste a variety of strange wild meats, things you never knew even existed, and certainly would not have eaten if you had known. I personally try to avoid anything that looks like meatballs. You could disguise a mess of night crawlers as meatballs and nobody would know the difference, unless you told them. And of course you have to tell the person that he has just eaten night-crawler meatballs, because that is half the fun of a wild dinner. At most wild dinners, therefore, I concentrate my own eating on dishes I think I recognize, most of which have labels on them, but the labels can't always be trusted. Usually, the person who prepared the dish is sitting nearby, watching his concoction as though it were bait, which it may well be.

"How do you like that?" he asks, grinning. "Pretty good, ain't it? My own private recipe."

"It's excellent," you say. "That's the best prairie chicken I ever ate."

"Ain't prairie chicken."

"Ain't? The label says prairie chicken."

"Label lies." At this the perpetrator of the falsely labeled dish bursts into raucous laughter, slapping his thigh with his hand while you contemplate slapping his head with a skillet of moose tongue.

"So what is it?" you ask.

"Fricasseed weasel! Har har har harrrrrreeeeeee!" He now almost faints from howling mirth.

"Oh, weasel, that's no big deal," you lie. "I've eaten weasel lots of times before."

"Not this part I bet you ain't!"

The joker now doubles over in sheer agony of mirth. People start rushing to his aid and asking what's wrong with old Joe.

"I don't know," you say, "probably something I ate."

Fortunately, I sometimes get invited to a wild dinner so classy, so fabulous, so unbelievable, that I am helpless to describe it. My friend Steve Runyon invited me to just such a dinner in Vancouver, Washington. Steve and several of his hunting and fishing buddies arranged for Chef Willy Madsen to prepare the dinner at a local restaurant from an assortment of wild fish and game they provided him. Now, Willy is no ordinary chef. He received his master's in the culinary arts at the International Hotel School in his native Denmark. He has worked as a chef in Denmark, Germany, Switzerland, Norway, the Far East, and West Africa. For many years, he was executive chef at the Portland Hilton, and since then has owned his own restaurants. His present specialty is hunt dinners such as the one I attended.

Before each course, Willy came out in his big chef's hat and described the treat that lay in store for us. I have since obtained a recording of his little pre-course talks, and I believe they capture the true essence and flavor of the dinner far better than I could. Here, then, is Willy Madsen, master chef, master of the wild dinner, and master human being:

Welcome to all of those of you that have not had dinner with me before. Let me give you a little background. This type of dining originated in Denmark at the place where I was apprentice a few seasons ago. You should know that you will find an absence of water and bread at the table. That you can have at home, it being just fill stuff. You should also know that nobody knows what the menu is except myself and the people who are serving you, so you are at my mercy. Everything that is served has been tried at one time or another. There is nothing so exotic that it hasn't been eaten at one place or another. Since you do not know what you are having, I shall come out between each course and tell you where the food originates from, how it's prepared, what's in it, even sometimes how to eat it. I also tell you about the wines that goes with it in the proper glasses, in lieu of the water.

You start with the first course being an interesting combination of game. You have mallards, pintails, and Canadian goose. They have all been roasted and the meat has been taken off the breast cage. A French pâté de foie gras has been formed over the breastbone. The breast meat has been sliced and put back on top of the pâté. With this you have a Cumberland Sauce and tiny pieces of toast. A very apropos starter will be a Royal Kir. A Royal Kir is a concoction of champagne and crème de cassis. This will be your first course. Enjoy yourself and have a nice evening and I shall return.

Course Two. This being a hunt dinner, there is nothing more appropriate than an old-fashioned Hunt Soup. We had venison bones and carcasses from pheasants that had been browned with vegetables and the proper spices and herbs. It has been simmered slowly and out of this we have arrived at a Hunt Soup Saint Hubert. Saint Hubert was the patron saint of the hunters. You will find in it pieces of venison, pieces of pheasants, vegetables, thyme, and cooked lentils and barley. The soup has been flavored slightly with sherry. With the soup you will have a glass of Hartley and Gibson Sherry Fino, a nice dry sherry. I'd like to suggest before you even start in on the soup to roll a little of the sherry in your mouth and then let the two marry together and you will have the best of two worlds.

This is your next course. One of you is an avid steelhead fisherman and on the Cowlitz River yesterday managed to catch a beautiful eleven-pound steelhead. We have prepared that in a typical Oregon manner. The steelhead has been deboned and butterflied and baked slowly with a light barbecue sauce and sprinkled with a white wine. With this we have a true saffron rice. The steelhead will be accompanied by a lovely, dry Chardonnay.

It is appropriate in good dining, after a fish course and before your entrée, to have a palate cleanser. I have through the years had my employees bring me in the early summer  all the roses that they can get from their parents' gardens. I take the rose petals and cook them slowly in a light sugar syrup and reduce it. What I basically do is come out with a rose perfume. This I mix with a little champagne and a little more sugar syrup and freeze the whole mess. What you basically have is a rose sorbet or rose sherbet, if you wish. To make sure that you do get the fish flavor out of your mouth, we will pop a bottle of champagne and float that on top.

This is your next course. A great hunter of the group has brought me a lovely leg of venison. I also got six lovely pheasants. The venison has been marinated in red wine, a little garlic and thyme, and has been slowly roasted and basted with the red wine, and from this, when the venison was roasted, we have derived a very lovely red wine sauce. The pheasants were first browned in butter and roasted slowly. Cream, whipping cream, was added to it and they were cooked in the cream with a little brandy. They have been deboned and the combination of the venison with the red wine and the cream sauce over the pheasant will be your next course. This is accompanied by brussels sprouts, cauliflower with chopped Oregon hazelnuts, carrots that have been cooked with a little oregano, and caramelized small potatoes. The wine we have is a Domaine St. George Cabernet Sauvignon. That should go excellent with these two dishes. That is your entrée.

I have been requested by Steve Runyon to come up with a good old-fashioned apple pie as he had at a previous dinner with us. My mother-in-law, Mabel Van Slyke, accommodated us and you will find an unusual, lovely, warm apple pie as your dessert. With that we have a large bowl of big balls of French vanilla ice cream. To accompany the apple pie à la mode we have chosen a fine Sandeman's Founders Reserve Port. The port should be a lovely addition to the apple pie. That is your dessert.

You will see in the background of the room in the corner that I have a coffee maker and a coffee grinder, which are my own personal. In the coffee grinder I have my own private blend of beans, which is roasted fresh weekly. I shall now make you a fresh-ground, good pot of coffee. With that an appropriate cordial to your own personal liking will be served.

Now that is what I call a wild dinner. So far it is the pinnacle of my avocation of eating, and I doubt it shall be equaled again, unless, of course, I get invited back to another of Willy Madsen's hunt dinners.

CHARLIE ELLIOTT COOKS

Charlie Elliott and I met at a bass-fishing tournament ten or so years ago and have been fast friends ever since. Charlie is a writer, with nearly twenty books and thousands of articles and short stories to his credit. He is well up into his eighties now and has started to slow down a bit. When he was seventy-five, he was still chasing bighorns around the Canadian Rockies, but now he restricts his hunting to quail and turkeys.

A Georgian, Charlie is a legend in hunting circles throughout the South and is widely known as "The Old Professor" in all matters related to the hunting of turkeys, the ultimate game, in Charlie's opinion. His great talent, however, is for the enjoyment of life. More than any person I've ever met, Charlie knows how to squeeze the last drop of nectar out of every single day that has been given to him, and a lot of days have been given to him. They couldn't have been given to a nicer guy, nor to anyone who knew how to put them to better use.

Among his many honors and distinctions is the fact that Charlie has never once even considered writing a cookbook, even though he is an expert on the cooking of food, both wild and domestic. He even taught me, a Yankee, how to eat grits. His one failure in life, however, is that he couldn't teach me to like them. I did manage to pry a couple of recipes out of him for this cookbook, one for duck and the other for catfish. They are as follows:

Charlie's Duck

Fillet duck breast from bone and slice into ¼-inch pieces. Sauté onion in bacon grease (4 slices bacon) and remove from skillet (bacon, too). Fry duck slices in a hot skillet for a minute on each side and sprinkle with Worcestershire sauce as it cooks. If you like your duck rare, as I do, serve immediately, with bacon and onions. If you like it well-done, put bacon, onions, and a couple tablespoons water back into skillet and simmer for 15 minutes with the lid on.

Charlie Elliott Cooks a Catfish

In Charlie's own words: "Location is important. Most desirable is forested shore of a slow-moving stream overcrowded with catfish.

"Time: Preferably during the first half of the night.

"Preliminary preparation: Before dark, set out a dozen more-or-less short poles tucked in bank above eddy water along shoreline. Poles are rigged with stout line, sinker to hold hook a foot or two off bottom, hook baited with chicken liver, grubs, worms, or other locally preferred catfish bait. Locate cooking arrangements near line of set hooks.

"Best cooking utensil is small (4–6 gallon) black cast-iron pot on three legs. Fill $\frac{1}{3}$ to $\frac{1}{2}$ full with lard, peanut oil, or vegetable shortening.

"Build fire around base of pot, preferably with 'lighter' knots or other resin-soaked wood for fast, hot fire. Cooking oil must be at exact temperature and kept at this same heat while cooking is done. Test oil when it begins to smoke. Testing is a simple procedure. Take a sip of "spirits" (corn likker or bourbon is best) and spit into pot. Cooking oil is right temperature when pot spits back at you.

"Catfish are taken off hooks, skinned, gutted, and beheaded. Coat lightly in batter made with cornmeal, eggs, water, and salt and pepper to taste. Place gently in smoking oil. Raw fish will sink to bottom. Cooked fish will rise to surface. For final test, remove fish from pot and stick with fork. If no steam escapes, fish is ready when cool enough to eat. Drain on absorbent towels.

"If set hooks, riverbank, cast-iron pot, and lighter knots are not available, same procedure may be followed on cookstove at home with smaller cooking pot. Remember that temperature must be exactly right. If guests are present and fastidious, dispatch them to bar or another part of house while you test the temperature."

VENISON ZUMBO

With the exception of me, my friend Jim Zumbo may be the best hunter and hunting writer in the country, probably in the world. I have taught him most of what he knows about hunting, but he will never admit it. That's the kind of guy he is. He is also an excellent cook. To capture the true flavor of Jim's cooking, you really must camp out with him in Idaho or Montana or Wyoming, where the dishes come well seasoned with bawdy jokes, loud laughter, bad whiskey, and endless psychological torment.

A few years ago, Jim and his gorgeous wife, Lois, succumbed to the lure of cookbook writing and came out with a dandy. Here is one of the Zumbos' favorite recipes.

Jim's Casserole Delight

from *The Venison Cookbook* by Jim and Lois Zumbo

2 pounds ground venison
2 tablespoons cooking oil
1/4 teaspoon garlic salt
1/2 teaspoon onion salt
1 can (10 1/2 ounces) condensed
   chicken noodle soup
1 can (10 1/2 ounces) condensed
   tomato soup
1/2 teaspoon chili powder
1/4 cup bottled taco sauce
1/2 teaspoon parsley flakes, or
   1 teaspoon finely cut fresh parsley
6 slices Monterey Jack cheese
   (1 × 3 × 1/4 inch), or Muenster
   cheese, if desired

In a large, heavy skillet, brown venison in oil, seasoning with garlic salt and onion salt as it cooks. When meat has lost all pink color, add the remaining ingredients except for the cheese. Mix lightly and transfer into a large casserole. Place cheese on top of mixture and bake for 30 minutes at 350° or until the meat mixture is hot and the cheese is melted. Serve on toast or rice. *Serves 4 to 6.*

Of all my hunting buddies, Bob Schranck comes closest to winning the title of master chef. On a book tour one time, I stopped over at his house in Minneapolis, where Bob prepared a feast of pheasant, grouse, quail, venison, wild rice, and I don't know what all. I think there was some duck, too, but I can't be sure, because I was in a delirium of devouring. Bob puts on wild-game cooking demonstrations on TV and around the country, he's that good. As with most of my hunting friends, Bob has written a cookbook, *Wild in the Kitchen*. After a shotgun or rifle or fishing rod, what every outdoorsman needs is this cookbook. It can be ordered directly from: Wild World Inc., 36 Western Terrace, Golden Valley, MN 55426, for $10.

Good bear recipes are harder to find than a good bear. I spent a week one night eating a bear steak. Actually, I ate only one bite. The more I chewed the bigger the bite got. By the time I gave up on it, the bite was the size of a yearling cub and still growing. I was starting to worry that it might come back to life. I could imagine the tabloid headline: BITE OF BEAR STEAK DEVOURS MAN. So anyway, here is a good recipe for bear from *Wild in the Kitchen*, in Schranck's own words:

Bob Schranck's Pressure-Cooked Corned Bear

"When we decided a game dinner would be a nice finale to a day of hunting grouse and woodcock on the Publisher Tom Nammacher's Pine Country acreage, it was a matter of scrounging up some additional things to go with the birds. We had some venison and a goose in the freezer. Then Bill Stevens came up with a bear roast. How could he cook it? Bear can be tough.

"No problem at all, since I had my trusty pressure cooker

at hand. It appeared that the gentleman who had supplied the bear roast had marinated it almost like a corned beef before he froze it. All I did was look up a recipe for cooking corned beef in the pressure cooker and we had our method. The result was a hit with the group.

"To corn the meat, combine 4 quarts hot water, 2 cups coarse salt, ¼ cup sugar, 2 tablespoons pickling spice, and 1½ teaspoons sodium nitrate or saltpeter. When the mixture cools, pour it over 4-pound bear roast which has been placed in deep enamel pot or stoneware jar. Add three cloves of garlic. Put a weight on the meat to keep it submerged, cover pot, and place in refrigerator to cure for 8 days. Turn meat every other day."

    4-pound corned bear roast
    2 cups water
    2 cloves garlic, chopped
    2 bay leaves
    2 small onions, sliced
    1½ cups celery, sliced

"Cover corned bear with cold water and let soak for 1 hour. Drain well. Use point of sharp knife to insert slivers of garlic into the roast about 1 inch deep. Place bear roast in pressure cooker on rack. Pour in water and add bay leaves, onions, and celery. Close cover securely and place pressure regulator on vent pipe. Cook 60 minutes at 15 pounds pressure. Let pressure drop of its own accord."

*S*teve Runyan and Gary Skordahl and their wives, Penny and Ann, conjure up wild meals the equal of those in a five-star restaurant. Here is one of their "field" recipes in Gary's words:

"We have yet to get comfortable with a name for this stew. Steve calls it 'Black Pot Stew,' and I call it 'Game Bag Stew.'

Those we feed it to call it 'Delicious Stew.' We think the magic is in the 14-quart, cast-iron Dutch oven. If you're not aware of it, a Dutch oven this size weighs 26 pounds. The lid weighs 12 of those pounds itself and has a rim that stands up about ³/₄ inch to keep the charcoal briquettes from rolling off when they are placed there for cooking. We use this recipe not only in camp but also in the living room, placing the Dutch oven in the fireplace."

Black Pot Game Bag Stew

UTENSILS:

1 14-quart Dutch oven
1 10-pound bag charcoal

INGREDIENTS:

2 to 3 game birds (pheasant, chukar, quail,
    or Huns, not to exclude a cottontail)
1 package dried onion soup mix
1 package brown gravy mix
3 to 4 large onions, cut in quarters
3 to 4 potatoes, chunked in cubes
2 to 3 carrots, chunked
1 to 2 green peppers, chunked
10 whole small-to-medium mushrooms
2 cups red wine (Personally I like lavender
    potatoes, so I fudge a little.)
Water to bring liquid to near top of veggies

INSTRUCTIONS:

Prepare fire pit or fireplace. Get charcoal going. Catch just the corners of the Dutch oven on rock or brick so the charcoal on the bottom won't be smothered. Load pot with ingredients and place on charcoal. Scoop up about 20 charcoal briquettes and place on the lid. Check veggies for doneness at 30 minutes; may take 40 minutes.

*H*ere's a somewhat less robust recipe from Steve and Gary. This recipe is perfect for game birds if they are shot up, because they can be thoroughly cleaned in the preparation for cooking.

Pheasant in Phyllo

2 tablespoons chopped onion
1 garlic clove, crushed
4 tablespoons butter
1 1/2 cups sliced mushrooms
1/2 cup whipping cream
4 breasts, boned, skinned and cut
   in small pieces
Phyllo
1/2 cup melted butter

Sauté onion and garlic in 2 tablespoons butter for a minute. Add 1/2 cup mushrooms and sauté for three minutes. Place in blender or food processor with whipping cream and puree.

In large frying pan, melt 2 tablespoons butter and sauté pheasant until done. Remove to a bowl.

Sauté remaining 1 cup mushrooms in same pan for 2 minutes. Drain pheasant and add pureed mixture and sautéed mushrooms; salt and pepper to taste. Cool and refrigerate.

Place a sheet of phyllo on counter and brush well with melted butter. Place second sheet on top and brush with butter also. Fold over in half. Brush with butter around border only.

Arrange small amount of mixture lengthwise on phyllo,

leaving a border. Fold in bottom edge of pastry, then sides, then over again. Place on baking sheet sprayed with Pam. Brush with melted butter.

Bake 425° for 15 to 20 minutes until golden brown.

*M*ae (formerly Russell) Van Derpas is one of the world-class ladies of Idaho. She is the mother of the infamous Russell clan: Bonnie, Jim, Ross, John, Dave, and Vivian. When the clan meets at Sandpoint each summer for a family reunion, the rest of the state shuts down and goes to Disneyland, just to get away from the racket. Some of the Russells are highly suspected of turning up as villainous characters in my stories. Jim and Ross are the two Russells I grew up hunting and fishing with. (I tried to grow up hunting and fishing with Bonnie and Vivian, but it never worked out.) It has been said of me that I'm "not too tightly wrapped." If that is so, it was Ross and Jim who undid the string. The odd thing is that their mother is one of the nicest and prettiest ladies I've ever had the good fortune to call a friend. Her husband, Pete, ain't bad either. Here is one of Mae's superb recipes—Tomato Soup Cake.

Mae's Tomato Soup Cake

Cream ½ cup butter, 1 cup sugar, 1 beaten egg, and mix thoroughly. Dissolve 1 teaspoon baking soda in 1 can of tomato soup. Add alternately with 1¾ cups flour sifted with 1 teaspoon cloves, 1 teaspoon cinnamon, ½ teaspoon nutmeg, ⅛ teaspoon salt. Mix thoroughly. Stir in 1 cup raisins, dates, or nuts. Bake in loaf pan, about 1 hour.

*H*ere is Ross Russell's method for stretching two grouse to feed the entire Russell clan.

Ross's Grouse Gravy

Heat 6 tablespoons Butter Crisco; add 3 tablespoons diced onion and two grouse breasts, boned, cubed, and floured. Fry until cooked. Remove from pan. Add 1 cup flour, 1 teaspoon salt, ½ teaspoon pepper. Stir and make roux and mix and cook until hot. Mix 1 can evaporated milk with 4 cups hot water and add in pan to roux. Stir until bubbly. Then add grouse and onions to pan. Serve over sourdough biscuits for breakfast. Can freeze to reuse.

*N*ow we come to my own recipes, which I have tested at great length.

Pat's Roast Wiener on a Willow Stick

1 wiener
1 bun or slice of bread
1 willow stick
1 fire
1 dog
1 Cub Scout

Cub Scout starts fire, then cuts willow approximately three feet long. Sharpens one end of willow and shaves off bark on a section the length of 1 wiener. Restarts fire. Removes 1 wiener from package. Drops wiener in sand. Wipes sand off wiener and onto Cub Scout uniform pants.

Restarts fire. Impales wiener lengthwise on pointed end of stick. Waits for fire to form flames. Dog walks by and licks wiener. Cub Scout cuffs dog on side of head with wiener and wipes dog hair off wiener onto uniform pants. Holds wiener over flame. Willow is too slender and droops wiener into ashes. Cub wipes wiener off on uniform pants. Controls droop of wiener to keep it in flames and out of ashes. Wiener begins to spurt juice and steam. Catches fire. Cub Scout blows out flames. Wiener is done. Cub inserts wiener in bun and eats.

Ubiquitous Onion-and-Celery-Soup Gravy

   1 can (10½ ounces) cream of celery soup
      (mushroom soup often substituted
      for celery soup)
   1 soup can water (or less)
   1 envelope dry onion soup

You don't need to brown the meat. Mix the ingredients and pour over venison steaks, duck breasts, pheasant—anything, and bake in moderate oven.

ELK CAMP GREEN HASH

After hunters have spent a week in elk camp, all food served turns out to be hash. Even bacon and eggs become hash, as do biscuits and gravy, fried potatoes and onions, pancakes and syrup, and other standard fare. Conversely, hash sometimes turns out to be bacon and eggs. A week in elk camp blurs fine distinctions. Sometime after the first week, the hash turns green and begins to look as if someone slept in it. This is normal. Eating green hash turns hunters green and helps them blend into the woods.

Keep green hash away from bears. Green hash defoliates bears, which is illegal in most states.

Check each spoonful of green hash carefully before you consume it. Try to determine if any parts are moving and, if so, whether they are hash or merely something just passing through.

Among the hunters eating green hash, one should be designated as "driver" and not be permitted to eat green hash. Make sure driver knows route to nearest emergency room. Do not attempt do-it-yourself stomach suction with gasoline siphon hoses that have not been rinsed in creek first.

Never sleep in enclosed tent with more than three hunters who have eaten green hash for supper. May be fatal. Some hunters take the precaution of keeping a caged canary in the tent with them. When the canary topples backward off its perch, it's time to get out of the tent.

But how do you make green hash, you ask? You do not "make" green hash. It occurs spontaneously after the first week of elk camp. Green hash increases in potency with each passing day. When it tries to crawl into the tent with you at night, it has become too potent and should be disposed of, either by striking it with an ax or shovel or by shooting it.

UNCLE RALPH'S LOGGING CAMP RECIPES

*M*y uncle Ralph Hanson was a marvelous cook. For most of his life, he ran kitchens in logging camps, clubs, and his own cafés. He cooked me my first hamburger when I was six years old, and he ran the lunch counter in a Priest River pool hall. It was an exciting moment for me. The place was packed with loggers and beautiful ladies, and I sat by myself on a high stool at the counter and watched Uncle Ralph cook my hamburger. It was a task he did not take lightly, nor did I. He deftly cut a portion from the great mound of raw burger, rolled it into a ball, and then pressed it out with his spatula into a perfectly round patty. At just the right moment, he flipped the patty over, and lay the two halves of a sliced bun on the grill to brown. He dabbed the top of the bun with a bit of hot grease to give it the proper sheen. Then he inserted the patty between the two halves of bun, put it on a plate with some slices of dill pickle, and served it to me. That hamburger, my first exotic food, was the best I've ever eaten.

Not long ago, my cousin Bud Hanson and his wife, Jo, came across Uncle Ralph's handwritten notebook of his logging-camp recipes. In case you happen to be operating a den for a dozen Cub Scouts or have a teenager in the house, here are a few of Uncle Ralph's logging-camp recipes.

Custard Pie

Egg-wash bottom crust
45 eggs. Whip well and add:
2¼ pounds sugar. Mix and add:
3 tablespoons vanilla
2 tablespoons nutmeg. Mix and add:
8 quarts milk and 1 quart milk mixed
   with 12 ounces cornstarch

Mix all together. Bake in moderate oven. *This batch will make about 14 pies.*

Vanilla Cake

4 pounds sugar
1½ pounds butter
1 tablespoon lemon extract. Cream and add:
1 quart egg yolks. Mix and add:
2 pints milk, 6 pounds flour mixed with:
3 ounces baking powder and
1 ounce cream of tartar. Mix well.

This cake will make paper sheets, sheet cakes, cupcakes, jelly roll, layer cake, macaroons. Just bake it.

Sandwich Filling

Mix cooked salad dressing with peanut butter, half of each. Combine it with shredded crisp cabbage, chopped raw carrots, and green pepper. Add a teaspoon of grated lemon and onion juice to moisten. Use only with cracked wheat or whole wheat bread.

Cupcakes

8 pounds sugar
1½ pounds butter and lard mixed. Mix and add:
11 eggs and vanilla extract. Mix and add:
8 pints milk. Mix and add:
2 level tablespoons baking powder mixed with
  enough flour to make dough

Makes 17 dozen.

White Cookies

2 quarts sugar
1 quart lard. Mix and add:
8 eggs. Mix and add:
1 quart milk
1 ounce lemon extract. Mix and add:
1 tablespoon baking powder mixed with flour enough to roll

This batch will make about 250 cookies.

Oatmeal Cookies

2 quarts sugar
1 quart lard. Mix well and add:
8 eggs. Mix and add:
1 tablespoon allspice
1 quart soaked currants
1 pint oatmeal. Mix and add:
1 quart milk and a little molasses.
   Mix and add:
4 tablespoons baking powder with enough flour to roll

This batch will make about 250 cookies.

Doughnuts

2½ pounds sugar
⅛ ounce mace
½ ounce salt. Mix and add:
10 eggs

$^1/_4$ ounce vanilla. Whip until frothy.
    Gradually pour in:
$^1/_2$ pound shortening. Add:
$2^1/_4$ quarts milk. Mix and add:
Enough flour to make a stiff dough,
    mixed with 4 ounces baking powder

Cut out and fry. *This batch makes about 200 doughnuts.*

Baking Powder Biscuits

Break 8 eggs in a bucket; add $^1/_2$ quart sugar and mix. Add 3 quarts milk and mix. Then put 7 quarts of sifted flour in mixing pan and add 6 ounces salt and 12 ounces baking powder and mix. Add wet ingredients. Before placing in oven, paint with cream. To double batch only add $1^1/_2$ quarts milk; other ingredients double except salt. *One batch makes 108 biscuits.*

*H*ere are two cures. The first is from Uncle Ralph's cookbook for hoarse throat. (He was much better at cooking than spelling.) The second is my own recipe, for curing that most deadly of all maladies, old age.

For Horse Throat

3 tablespoons vinegar, 2 tablespoons sugar, 1 walnut of butter, boil until like syrup. Drink when cool enough.

CURE FOR OLD AGE

A dozen years ago, when my mother was well up into her seventies, Troll came up with one of her ill-conceived ideas for a camping trip. Her family and mine would meet at a large lake in Canada, where we would rent a boat and ferry across to a river that Troll had heard offered fantastic fishing. "It'll be fun," Troll said persuasively if somewhat less than prophetically. Being feeble of mind at the time, I agreed to engage in this insanity.

Then Mom heard about the adventure, and insisted upon going along. There was no point wasting time trying to dissuade her. Even though she was now old and barely able to totter about, once she said she was going to do something, she did it, and any further discussion was futile.

"Surely you don't plan to sleep out on the hard cold ground," I said. "At your age, that could kill you."

"Of course I won't sleep out," she said. "I'll just rent a cabin at the resort. Then you can take me over to the camp during the day and bring me back at night."

"Sounds good, Mom," I said. "It's only about five miles across the lake. Let's see, two round-trips for me, that will add up to a total of about twenty miles a day of boat driving. At my age, that could kill me."

"I knew you'd see it my way."

Early on the fateful day, my wife, Bun, and I picked up Mom at her house. Bun helped pull the shawl up around Mom's shoulders, because it was a little cool out. "Thank you, dear," Mom said in the quavery old-lady voice she had adopted in recent years. Bun and I took Mom by the arms as we helped her down the porch step and steadied her as she tottered to the car.

"It's a two-hour drive to the lake," I said. "I hope it won't tire you out too much."

"Oh, I'll survive."

We arrived at the lake a little before noon. It was a cliché summer day: warm and sunny without a cloud in the sky. The lake looked like blue-tinted glass, it was so smooth and gentle and lovely. It appeared even larger than I had expected. I noticed some shrubs on the mountain across the lake and asked

a local fisherman what kind they were. "Pine trees," he said. "Oh," I said.

The boat-rental place had only one size boat available: aluminum twelve-footers with five-horse outboards. "I'll wait until something larger comes in," I told the boat-rental man.

"Okay," he said.

"How long do you suppose that will be?"

"About two years. That's when we buy some fourteens."

The Troll and her family and my kids had already crossed the lake in the twelve-footers. I didn't see any reason I couldn't do the same.

"How long to cross the lake in one of these boats?" I asked the man.

"Twenty minutes."

"Really?"

"An hour."

"That's what I thought. Any chance of hitting a storm halfway across on a nice day like this?"

"Naw."

"Really?"

"Some."

I turned to Mom. "Well, Bun and I will get you squared away in your cabin, fix some lunch, and then head across. I'll be back to pick you up tomorrow to come over and spend the day."

"Oh, it's so nice today," Mom said, "I think I'll go over with you now, and you can bring me back this evening."

"But . . ."

"Help me into the boat, dear."

Half an hour later we were out in the middle of the lake, with Mom up in the bow, Bun amidship, and me hunched over the little five-horse, wringing every fraction of a knot out of it. In the great expanse of water, however, we hardly seemed to be moving. The motor howled unnervingly every time we pitched over the crest of a wave. The storm had hit us twenty minutes out from shore.

Mom disappeared beneath a wave that had just crashed over the bow. She reappeared a second later, clinging to the gunnels with both hands.

"Wow!" she cried. "That was a big one!"

Bun bailed frantically. Our hats blew off in the wind. We bucked over the top of another wave and slid endlessly down into the trough, and came crashing up through the crest of another wave.

"Keep her headed into the waves!" Mom roared. "You're taking on too much water! Stop fooling around and pay attention to what you're doing!"

"I'm doing the best I can," I yelled back, trying to wipe the spray from my glasses so I could see.

"Well, it isn't good enough," Mom yelled back. "Head for the lee of that point. The water's calmer there."

"What point?"

"Off to your left! Goose that motor up some more! We're hardly making any headway in this wind!"

Bad enough we're all about to die in a storm, I thought, but my mother suddenly has to rejuvenate and take command.

At last we swept in toward a rocky shore. While we were still in two feet of water, Mom vaulted over the gunnel and waded ashore, pulling the bowline. While we sat out the storm, she stripped off her soaked bloomers and tied them to the end of a stick. She sat on a rock in high spirits, watching the waves crash against the shore. There was nothing my mother loved more than a good calamity.

Presently, Mom grew impatient waiting for the storm to ease up to a mere tempest and insisted that we put out again, to cruise down the shoreline in search of Troll's camp. I had hoped she would at least wait until I had knitted the ends of my nerves back together, but there was no point in begging for mercy. Mom sat in the bow, holding the stick overhead with her bloomers whipping in the wind like a flag of triumph.

When we at last found the Troll's camp, Mom again vaulted into the water and waded ashore, cheerfully waving her flag. The awaiting family stared at her in disbelief and not a little dismay. This camping trip was about to be shaped up.

That night Mom slept on the hard cold ground and arose early next morning full of vim and vigor. Everyone else was swollen with mosquito bites, but my mother had not a single bite. She simply wouldn't put up with having something so inconsequential as a mosquito bite her. As soon as she had ordered the fires built and laid out the breakfast menu, she sat down on a log, rested her hands on her knees, and surveyed the situation. "Shoot," she said. "I'm not going to rent any cabin. Waste of good money. I'm going to stay here and camp with the rest of you. This is fun!"

That camping trip added twenty years to my mother's life, and took ten off my own. I now knew why old people are locked up in retirement and nursing homes. If we took them out into storms and on camping trips, we'd never be rid of them.

Years later, Mom said to me, "Pat, why don't you write a humorous story about the time we crossed that lake in a storm?"

"Because I still don't think it was funny, Mom. Maybe in another twenty years or so, it'll seem funny to me, but so far it doesn't."

"Well, I want you to write that story."

Okay, okay. There it is, Mom.

Index